THE BREXIT CHRONICLES

Tales of Treachery and Skulduggery

PAUL McQUEEN

Published by
Graystone LA
Tanner Business Center
Chew Valley Road
Oldham OL3 7NH
United Kingdom

www.brexitchronicles.uk
www.g-la.co.uk

ISBN: 978-1-9164969-5-8

First Edition

A catalogue record for this book is available from the British Library

Copyright © Paul McQueen 2020

DAVID CAMERON GOT IT RIGHT

There's nothing to apologize for David, because you got it right.

Over the past 100 years, treaty after treaty was signed off through the British Parliament. Our EU neighbours held referendum after referendum whereas successive British governments did not. One was long overdue.

For the first time in 40 years David Cameron gave the British people a say about EU membership.

THE CRUX OF IT

It was the right thing to do and 72.2% of the British public agreed with it. This was an unusually high turnout with some 33,577,342 people exercising their right to vote.

The Brexit Chronicles reveals the whole EU saga by following a timeline, backed up by videos of key speeches and newsreels from the decision makers in power. The EU has always been an emotional roller-coaster ride for politicians and public alike.

Start at the beginning of this book as you won't want to miss any of the tales of treachery and skulduggery leading up to the Brexit betrayal.

After reading The Brexit Chronicles you will certainly be better informed, but you may not like what you hear.

18 THINGS THIS BOOK COVERS

1. A timeline of key-events joining the dots leading up to Brexit.

2. Do you know what the EU is about and who it benefits most?

3. What is ‚CAP' and why is it important to France?

4. How much influence does Germany really have over the EU?

5. Get interactive with 140 hours of original footage online.

6. Read the incident then click to view speeches of the day.

7. Was the public really well informed in the 2016 referendum?

8. Britain was the second country to vote Leave. Who was first?

9. Understand why MPs really don't want a second referendum.

10. Find out why a planned UK referendum had to be cancelled.

11. Is there a difference between democracy and 'EU democracy'?

12. Who said, 'there is a tradition of not holding referendums'?

13. Do you remember the 'Respect the Irish Vote' campaign?

14. On which five occasions could Brexit have been avoided?

15. Major policy changes over 45 years. How many referendums?

16. Cameron's defining moment, after which there was no return.

17. How much did the UK pay the EU in 2018?

18. With the cards stacked in favour of Remain, why did they fail?

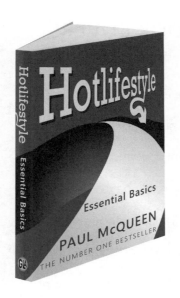

Hotlifestyle - Essential Basics

ISBN 978-1-9164969-0-3

The Essenital Guide for Getting Your Life on Track

Creating a real competitive edge in your life requires an effective routine and making better choices. This is the only book to cover all the bases leading to a healthier happier richer you.

www.Hotlifestyle.info

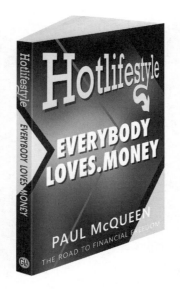

Everybody Loves Money

ISBN 978-1-9164969-3-4

The Best Handbook for Dealing with Money Matters

These 224 pages are packed with practical, actionable tips to lift your personal finances up to the next level. Take back control, keep a grasp on your hard-earned cash and start working towards financial independence.

www.EverybodyLoves.Money

TIMELINE

When it comes to Brexit,
now nobody is impartial.

~ Paul McQueen

PREFACE

Simply mentioning the 'B' word provokes an extreme emotional response in everyone I talk to. Everybody has an opinion on the subject, to the point that they are simply compelled (obsessed) to share it with me. It has polarized a nation, to the extent that it seems every facet of life is now seen in terms of Leave or Remain. Political parties, newspapers, television programmes are all one or the other. Unbiased media is a thing of the past. The 2016 referendum has torn apart families and friends, and tormented some to the point of murder (MP Jo Cox). Brits, famous for calm, stiff upper lips, and tolerance have become a nation of ranting protesting revolutionaries with an 'if you're not with us, then you're against us attitude'. Like two tribes going to war any amount of treachery and skulduggery is acceptable, as long as it helps to win. Whatever happened to that sense of fairness, correctness, and justice that, in my opinion, separated us Brits from every other nation? Or have we just forgotten these values?

So, on 23 June 2016 it happened. Much to the surprise of those who were campaigning for Brexit, they actually won. I understand that Boris Johnson went to bed on the evening of the 23rd resolved that he had done his best but was defeated. After all, our leaders and the polls were very clear, the Remain vote would win.

The next day, I had this crazy notion that Leave meant Leave, and that MPs would suppress their own bias to pursue the will of the people. After all, this is not Somalia or Mexico we're talking about, this is Britain for god's sake! You'd think that our elected lawmakers should be able to step up to the mark. As we have seen, this has sadly not been the case as each MP has jockeyed for position to pursue their own Brexit leaning.

By my estimate, 80% of all MPs on both sides of the House are for Remain. This creates a huge dilemma. Consider, that 70% of Labour constituencies voted for Brexit but you have Labour leader Jeremy Corbyn announcing that 'Labour will become the Remain Party'. You can see the problem.

Watching Cllr Luisa Porritt MEP (Lib-Dems) holding a Stop Brexit banner and spouting how Boris Johnson is flouting democracy, demonstrates the hypocrisy of elected politicians who show little respect for a decision made by the people.

 brexitchronicles.co.uk/br/LM

I have always been interested to know what motivates people to behave in a certain way. What makes people tick? Why do some find life hard and others seem to glide through it with ease? Why do some people make bad choices at times when they should go far? Why do people shoot themselves in the foot? To this end I began to author a series of books around lifestyle choices. Writing the Hotlifestyle series made me ask, why would 21 Members of Parliament choose to vote against their own party and constituents, knowing full well that the consequences would be dismissal. Long-serving MPs who have enjoyed top positions in their party have chosen to throw their career away because of Brexit.

Was there so much conflict in the mind of MP Jo Johnson (brother of Boris), that he had no other alternative but to quit politics altogether? Never have we seen people so emotionally charged about a subject that they behave irrationally, so great is their pain and so deep is their passion. It seems that when it comes to Brexit nobody is impartial.

The Remainers have totally taken control of the narrative since the referendum, feeling cheated as the clear outcome promised by the polls failed to materialize. The media are playing their part in fuelling the conflict as it makes a great story and helps sell more newspapers.

The treachery and skulduggery of the media and our lawmakers post-referendum has made a laughing stock of the UK around the world. They have dumped on the very principles that made this country great.

This seems to be the plan

Drag out and frustrate the Brexit process to a point where the general public will agree to anything just to make it go away.

The Brexit Story - 43 Years in the Making

The Brexit story began long before the 2016 referendum. It was on the table just one year after Great Britain joined the, then, Common Market in 1974. The 1975 in-out referendum went in favour of Remain and, although the result was different, there are striking similarities between the actions of Prime Minister Harold Wilson and David Cameron's more recent tactics. Comparisons can also be drawn with Britain's fundamental ,problems' with European integration.

The Brexit Chronicles is about those people whose wholehearted belief in a vision of a United States of Europe experienced a massive setback. About leaders who set a course to unification but who failed to involve the general public in the decision-making process. About a public who are just as divided about Europe as they were in 1975.

Let me walk you down the corridors of power as the plot to bring a, mostly unwilling, nation into the fold gathers momentum, only to fail 43 years on. I want to highlight the events and key players that formed the opinions of a nation.

The Brexit saga has never been put together chronologically before in a format giving the clearest insight into what happened.

I will be naming names and quoting from those in power to reveal who told the truth, who prophesied the end game and who simply made an ass of themselves.

I'm very concerned by the way our view of current affairs is distorted by a mainstream media that relies so heavily on speculation. Perhaps we should redefine the word 'news' since today it is 10% information and 90% speculation.

THE BOTTOM LINE

Speculation is not news.

Let's take an in-depth look at the critical moments and the opinion makers who led us down this path. Let's expose the broken promises, deceit, and hypocrisy from all those who, too often, omitted the pieces of information that didn't suit their own bias. Whether you're in the Remain or the Leave camp, reading this book will give you a truly informed view of why we are where we are today. This is a balanced, honest catalogue of Britain's path to leaving the EU.

There's a wonderful example from 1985 of a talk show with the late, great Kenneth Williams (of Carry On fame) and an audience who were just as divided and emotional as people are today. A Labour MEP explains why he is a Eurosceptic. Williams, a staunch Remainer, is very well informed and shows more knowledge on the subject than the two MEPs sitting next to him. A demonstration that discussion of Britain's EU membership has been a bone of contention for a very long time.

Let's Look at Three European Union Institutions

It's important from the onset to have a basic understanding of the workings of the three main institutions (there are seven in total) that drive the EU:

➤ The European Commission

➤ The European Council

➤ The European Parliament

Each body operates independently and has a President. These Presidents are the main players in driving and controlling EU policy.

The European Commission (EC)

The European Commission is made up of one representative from each member state, usually an ex-high-ranking politician. The commissioners are responsible for drafting laws and treaties and can propose new legislation. They ensure that EU laws and treaties are obeyed, which is why the Commission is also known as the Guardian of the Treaties.

Past EC Presidents you might recognize are José Manuel Barroso (EPP) (2004-2014), Jean-Claude Juncker (EPP) (2014-2019) and Ursula von der Leyen (EPP) (2019-2024). (EPP - The 'European People's Party' is the largest political group of MEPs within the European Parliament.) The EC is by far the most powerful of the three institutions, which is why it's important to have the right person as President. The Treaty of Lisbon states that Presidents are chosen by the Council and then presented to the European Parliament for approval.

The European Council (EUCO)

Members of this exclusive club are current heads of state or government of the EU member states. They are often seen sitting at a large round table at summits, where they agree the EU's overall political direction and priorities. The EC President also sits at the table with the EUCO President.

EUCO Presidents have been ex-politicians, like Herman Van Rompuy (EPP) (2009-2014), Donald Tusk (EPP) (2014-2019) and Charles Michel (ALDE) (1 December 2019 - 31 May 2022).

The European Parliament (EP)

The European Parliament is currently made up of 751 Members of the European Parliament (MEPs), voted in by 400 million people in elections held every five years. It is the only EU institution that is directly elected, but no legislation is made in the EP. The EP President is elected by the MEPs and a term lasts 2.5 years. They chair debates and oversee all the activities of the Parliament. It is mainly an administrative role but holds a similar position to that of Speaker in the House of Commons.

Presidents are usually politicians who became MEPs, Hans-Gert Pöttering (2007-2009), Antonio Tajani (2017-2019) and David-Maria Sassoli (S&D) (July 2019 - December 2021).

BOOK ONE

THE COMMON MARKET YEARS

(1958 - 1992)

INTRODUCTION

Tales of Treachery and Skulduggery

One of the most important questions of this era is, why doesn't Britain sign the 1957 Treaty of Rome (along with the six original members of France, West Germany, Belgium, Italy, Luxembourg, and the Netherlands) that creates the European Economic Community (EEC)?

In hindsight it's easy to criticize, but had Britain been instrumental in the formation of EEC policies from the very beginning it would have had more say in the make-up of the treaty. Especially with regard to the Common Agricultural Policy (CAP), which is slanted in favour of France.

CAP policies, together with the supranational nature of the treaty, make Britain pull out of negotiations. So it is Britain's choice not to participate in the talks leading up to the signing of the Treaty of Rome. And not for the first time.

During negotiations in 1951 with France and Germany on the European Coal and Steel Community (predecessor to the Treaty of Rome), Britain also withdraws from talks when the supranational nature of the treaty is defined.

In the 1950s Britain is a global economic powerhouse in its own right through established trading channels with its colonies and the British Commonwealth (Canada, Australia, New Zealand, South Africa, India, Pakistan, Sri Lanka, Irish Free State, and Newfoundland). It also enjoys a special relationship with the United States.

Britain has its own agenda for pursuing a 'one-world economic system' policy with the pound sterling as the central currency, English as the language, and Britain at the centre of a flourishing 'empire'.

The British government believes in tariff-free trade. If tariffs are to be applied then each country should decide independently with whom and by how much – in contrast to the policies of the EEC, with its centralized system for tariffs run from Brussels. This means the EEC dictating the tariffs Britain could charge on Commonwealth imports, if it joins.

The Commonwealth grew out of a British Empire that held sway over a quarter of the world's population by 1922 (about 458 million people)– it grew significantly throughout the 1970s and can boast a total of 53 countries today. An image of the British monarch still appears on money and stamps in many Commonwealth countries and English is widely spoken.

Europe, still recovering economically from World War II, has very little to offer in the way of trade with Britain, who is putting its future into building the Commonwealth.

In a famous 1946 speech Winston Churchill says: 'The position of Britain was to support European integration, especially between Germany and France, since it was a solid way to avoid future wars on the continent.'

Churchill later comments that, 'Britain should have been a friend of European integration, but never a part of it.'

France and Germany are the dominant force in Europe during the 1950s and experience a rapid recovery after World War II, partly due to the implementation of the Marshall Plan.

The Marshall Plan, a US initiative started in 1948, donated over $12 billion (the equivalent of nearly $100 billion in 2019 terms) in US aid to help rebuild war-torn economies. The largest recipient of aid by far was the United Kingdom (about 26% of the total), followed by France (18%), and West Germany (11%). The rest went to 18 other European countries involved in World War II.

After refusing to sign an agreement with the EEC the British then opt for a new organization based on a free trade area without any form of supranational ambition. In January 1960 the Treaty of Stockholm is signed, and the European Free Trade Association (EFTA) is founded, creating a free trade area for industrial goods. Party to the treaty are: Great Britain, Denmark, Sweden, Norway, Portugal, Austria, Ireland, and Switzerland.

Move on a year to 1961 and the world has already changed significantly. Europe is growing faster than Britain and the government of the day fears diplomatic and economic exclusion from Europe.

Only on a third attempt is Britain able to join the EEC. It has no influence on policy as the Treaty of Rome is already established and the six founding members will not adapt it to appease those now wanting to be part of their club. Any new member has to accept all EEC communitarian policies, not just some.

It's a bad deal right from the start as signatories can't assess what financial damage the CAP might inflict on Britain.

Eleven years later Margaret Thatcher remedies this unfair practice, to some extent; only for the remedy to be given away by a later Prime Minister.

> *The Brexit saga begins with the signing of the Treaty of Rome*

CHAPTER ONE

Walking the Dinosaur

March 1957 - Signing the Treaty of Rome

The signing of the Treaty of Rome by six member states (France, West Germany, Belgium, Italy, Luxembourg, and the Netherlands) creates the European Economic Community (EEC) - or the Common Market as it is referred to in Britain.

The treaty comes into force on 1 January 1958. It seeks to reduce customs duties, create a common agricultural policy (CAP), a common transport policy, and a European social fund among member states. It is without question one of the most important treaties ever to be drafted and implemented anywhere in the world – and the CAP is central to it.

The CAP - from a British aspect

Farming is a challenging business that depends on many factors for success, including weather, climate, supply and demand, and pest control. France has 20% of its workforce engaged in farming and pushes early on for policies that promote the interests of their farming industry.

The French government, led by Charles de Gaulle (1959–1969), is supported heavily by French farmers, which means keeping them happy to remain in power, which means keeping food prices artificially high. France's agricultural sector is five times bigger than Britain's, so a CAP is an important factor in any treaty France is party to.

Only general principles for a CAP are approved in the Treaty of Rome. Details are delayed by many years, until de Gaulle's lobbying forces other members to sign up to it. De Gaulle doesn't want the UK to join the EEC until the CAP is approved by the six founding members. He knows the British will want to limit the detrimental consequences of this policy as it is not in Britain's interests.

The CAP is based on enforcing fair food prices (for farmers), together with tariffs on imported foods from non-ECC countries, to ensure no undercutting.

Britain, with its relatively small farming sector, is heavily reliant on cheap food imports from the Commonwealth and other countries. British farmers are also subsidised by the tax payer as part of a British cheap food trade policy. Not one of the original six EEC members has anything like the benefits that Britain enjoys through association with the Commonwealth.

There are two main CAP principles:

1. All EEC members should be treated equally - meaning Britain cannot be given preferential treatment by allowing tariff-free imports from outside the EEC.

2. EEC members should be treated better than non-EEC members - meaning only food bought from within the EEC is tariff free.

THE BOTTOM LINE

The common agricultural policy ensures higher prices for the consumer, subsidies to farmers, and duties on imports from non-EEC countries.

The British policy of tariff-free imports from the Commonwealth and subsidies to British farmers creates the cheap food trade policy.

These opposing policies are not compatible with one another and the six EEC members refuses to compromise during negotiations. They say it is up to Britain to adopt all the policies of the EEC if they want to join. This means that Britain would be forced to introduce tariffs on all imports from Commonwealth countries.

The six founding members of the EEC cannot allow a new member preferential treatment over suppliers from within the EEC. In real terms this means a rise in the cost of living through ending the cheap food policy, buying more expensive food from Europe, and taxing non-EEC imports so as not to undermine European farmers.

Even with a levy on imports from the Commonwealth, France thinks there is still an incentive for Britain to bring in food from outside the EEC, that of benefiting from import duties. So, during Britain's initial negotiations, the six members create a new budgetary policy in reply to: 'What was to happen with monies collected through import duties?' The answer is simple.

Send the money collected in levies to Brussels

The original six EEC members decide that all import taxes will be sent to the European Agricultural Guidance and Guarantee Fund (EAGGF), set up in 1962 in Brussels. The fund will distribute the money to member states, in proportion to the size of their agricultural sector.

Who benefits the most from this arrangement?

The country with the largest agriculture sector, namely France. Any other subsidising of farmers by individual countries will not be allowed.

This means that due to Britain's small agricultural sector it would be paying the most in but getting the least out, making Britain the second largest contributor to the fund within two years of joining.

French farmers benefiting from large subsidies due to British taxes paid directly into Brussels allow rapid modernization of the farming sector to take place. Meanwhile British farmers have their subsidies cut, stifling their growth, and puts an end to the cheap food trade policy.

The British rebate demanded by PM Margaret Thatcher in June 1984 is an attempt to remedy this unfair practice.

October 1959 - Conservative Party wins election

The third consecutive victory for the Conservative Party, now led by Prime Minister Harold Macmillan (1957–1963). Boosted by strong economic growth, the election is fought on the slogan 'You've never had it so good'. Britain is faring well just 14 years after the end of World War II.

Margaret Thatcher (Con) is also elected MP for Finchley and takes her seat in the House of Commons for the very first time.

May 1960 - Trade bloc EFTA established

Iceland, Liechtenstein, Norway, and Switzerland create the European Free Trade Association (EFTA) as an alternative trade bloc for those unable, or unwilling, to join the EEC. The Stockholm Convention (EFTA treaty) is signed on 4 January 1960 by seven countries, including Britain.

July 1961 - Negotiations begin to join the EEC

The United Kingdom, Ireland, and Denmark open negotiations to join the EEC. The British Conservative PM, Harold Macmillan, is watching the EEC very closely as growth in Europe exceeds that in Britain. He is worried about being excluded and wants to be part of a, now booming, Europe.

January 1963 - Britain's application to join vetoed

Britain's first attempt to join the EEC is thwarted by French President Charles De Gaulle, who fears that it could open the door to unwanted influence from America. He views Britain's membership of the EEC as potentially destabilizing. The CAP is not yet ratified by the EEC.

Here is a newsreel of the day, reporting on De Gaulle's blocking of Britain's entry and citing that France looks forward to being the dominant force within the Common Market.

 brexitchronicles.co.uk/mc/DG

October 1963 - Macmillan resigns as PM

Macmillan uses a terminal cancer diagnosis to immediately resign as Prime Minister and retires from politics. In September 1964 he takes up the chairmanship of his family's publishing business – Macmillan Publishers – lives a further 23 years and dies at the ripe old age of 92.

October 1964 - Labour Party narrowly win election

The Labour Party beats the Conservatives by only four seats at the general election. Harold Wilson becomes Prime Minister (1964–1970 and again in 1974–1976). First on the agenda is dealing with an inherited deficit of £800 million.

March 1966 - Labour Party win by a landslide

Wilson calls a snap election after only 17 months in government because of his four-seat majority. It pays off. He now commands a massive 98-seat majority in the House.

The Scottish National Party (SNP) still has no seats in Parliament, despite 23 candidates standing.

March 1966 - Decimalization announced to Parliament

Chancellor of the Exchequer James Callaghan announces to Parliament the intention to introduce decimalization. Although it has been discussed in Britain since 1847 the government decides to act fairly quickly after the election, aware that joining the Common Market will raise food prices due to CAP tariff policies.

The currency system of pounds, shillings, and pence, in which one pound is equal to 240 pennies, would be converted to one pound equalling 100 new pence.

The old pound note (a quid, written as £1) was worth 240 pennies. The ten-shilling note (or ten bob, written as 10s or 10/-) was worth 120 pennies and the shilling (a bob, written as 1s or 1/-) was worth 12 pennies (written as 12d).

The Decimal Currency Board (DCB) is created to manage the transition by 15 February 1971, called D-day.

Those who experience the switch to decimal currency say things get more expensive. Inflation is about 9% when the new money is introduced and, despite everything, prices begin to soar after February 1971.

James Callaghan gives an enthusiastic interview to explain the benefits of decimalization. Its cost to industry is around £128 million and £23.5 million to the government − £1 million of that for advertising and publicity.

↳ brexitchronicles.co.uk/mc/dec

Was decimalization a ploy to confuse the public in anticipation of Common Market membership?

November 1967 - Sterling devalued on Black Monday

To address a mounting deficit Chancellor of the Exchequer James Callaghan reluctantly devalues sterling by 14% to make imports more expensive and exports cheaper. This causes inflation to rise.

↳ brexitchronicles.co.uk/cm/BM

November 1967 - Second attempt to join EEC vetoed

Labour PM Harold Wilson's attempt to join the EEC is vetoed again by the President of France. Charles de Gaulle says that Britain harbours a 'deep-seated hostility' to any pan-European project and that 'Economy, working practices and agriculture made Britain incompatible with Europe'.

The five members who do support Britain's entry are warned that if they try to impose British membership on France it would result in the break-up of the community.

July 1969 - French President supports UK application

France's new President, Georges Pompidou (1969–1974, elected on a pro-European manifesto) wants to enlarge EEC membership. His initiative is supported by member states at the Hague EEC summit conference. Leaders agree to open negotiations with four applicant countries: Great Britain, Ireland, Denmark, and Norway.

Only after France ensures that other countries will subsidise her farming sector through CAP, do they actively pursue British entry. Britain will be forced to impose levies on imports of food from the Commonwealth, the proceeds of which will go direct to the EAGGF in Brussels to fund the CAP.

THE CRUX OF IT

Britain will, in effect, be handing over money it collects to subsidise French farmers and will simultaneously provide them with a market for their surplus.

June 1970 - Conservatives win election by a landslide

The Conservative Party, led by Edward (Ted) Heath, surprisingly defeats the ruling Labour Party in a general election. They win 330 seats to 228, compared to the last election's 253 to 364 for Labour. A swing in the country's mood loses Labour, led by Harold Wilson, a massive 77 seats and ends 13 years of Labour rule.

The opinion polls predicted a comfortable Labour victory with at least a 12% lead over the Conservatives. The polls completely underestimated how devaluing the pound, coupled with inflation and high interest rates, would damage Labour's credibility.

Ted Heath is a strong supporter of the EEC and sets out to negotiate Britain's entry. But his tenure is marked by major industrial strikes and high inflation.

CHAPTER TWO

Britain Joins the Common Market

January 1972 - Signing the Treaty of Accession

On the third attempt, and after years of negotiation, Britain joins the EEC without consulting the people. Ireland and Denmark join at the same time, after holding a referendum. Norway's referendum goes against joining. That's right, four countries are invited to join the EEC; three hold a referendum and Britain doesn't.

UK Prime Minister Edward Heath, leader of the Conservative Party (1970-1974), signs a Treaty of Accession in Brussels on 22 January 1972. It is to take effect on 1 January 1973.

So, here's a peculiarity of politics.

First sign the treaty, then get parliamentary approval.

An Act of Parliament is required for the Treaty to take effect since no referendum has been held. So, four days after Heath signs the Treaty, the European Communities Act 1972 is being read in parliament.

January 1972 - The European Communities Act 1972

22 January 1972 - Treaty of Accession signed in Brussels.

26 January 1972 - Bill introduced to the House of Commons by MP Geoffrey Rippon for the first time.

17 February 1972 - The second reading isn't getting much support. The Conservatives have a free vote, meaning each MP can vote as they see fit. Labour uses the whip to vote the Bill down, which some 70 MPs ignore and vote for the Bill anyway.

Here is part of Heath's speech to the House of Commons:

'I believe that our friends (the EEC) would find it incomprehensible if we were to tear up the agreement - the very agreement we have struggled for more than a decade to achieve. For years to come they would understandably ask whether any trust could be placed in Britain's role in any future international agreements. Our influence in world monetary and trade discussions would be destroyed. These questions would be settled by the United States, the European Community and Japan. The Community would not be broken up if we were to defect. It would suffer a bitter shock, but it would survive and go on. But Britain would not benefit from the progress it was making.' 'I have dealt with many of the major issues raised in the debate. I will deal now in particular with one matter. As the House knows, I have always believed that our prosperity and our influence in the world would benefit from membership. I believed until recently that we could carry on fairly well outside, but I believe now that with developments in world affairs, and the speed at which they are moving, it will become more and more difficult for Britain alone.'

'Faced with this prospect of change, I do not believe that any Prime Minister could come to this House and say, "We have secured the chance to join the European Community; we have signed the Treaty of Accession; we have the opportunity of full membership; but I now advise this House to throw them away." I do not believe that any Prime Minister could say that, and it follows from what I have said that this Bill is not a luxury which we can dispense with if need be.'

'It has been a central policy of three successive governments, irrespective of party, and of all three main parties in this House that Britain should join the European Community if suitable arrangements could be negotiated. By a large majority this House decided in principle last October that Britain should join the Community on the basis of the arrangements negotiated by my Right Honourable and learned friend the Chancellor of the Duchy. Any Government which thereafter failed to give legislative effect to that clear decision of this House would be abdicating its responsibilities.'

'I must tell the House that my colleagues and I are of one mind that the Government cannot abdicate their responsibilities in this matter. Therefore, if this House will not agree to the Second Reading of the Bill tonight and so refuses to give legislative effect to its own decision of principle, taken by a vast majority less than four months ago, my colleagues and I are unanimous that in these circumstances this Parliament cannot sensibly continue. I urge Honourable Members to implement the clear decision of principle taken on 28th October last and to cast their votes for the Second Reading of this Bill.'

MPs vote narrowly, by 309-301, in favour of the Bill

In this June 1972 interview with Ted Heath it is clear that the country is in a mess. After two years in power the problems are mounting. Prices are rising due to high inflation. High pay settlements as a result of strikes and mass unemployment are prevalent.

When it comes to joining the EEC, a poll suggests that the public are either indifferent or hostile. Heath is of the opinion that the polls are wrong, and believes the public are in favour of joining.

He is asked about the vote in Parliament on the European Communities Act 1972 and gives the impression that an overwhelming number of MPs voted it in.

 brexitchronicles.co.uk/mc/eca

13 July 1972 - The third and final reading of the bill; MPs vote 301-284 in favour; it then passes to the House of Lords and receives Royal Assent on 17 October 1972.

> **MPs vote in favour of the Bill by
> a narrow margin of 301-284**

THE BOTTOM LINE

The Bill to ratify joining the EEC is passed by only 17 votes on the third reading.

Was there a case for a referendum?

Edward Heath knows of EEC intentions

Edward Heath confirms that he was aware of EEC intentions to become a United States of Europe:

'The community which we are joining is far more than a common market. It is a community in the true sense of that term. It is concerned not only with the establishment of free trade, economic and monetary union and other major economic issues ...'. Ted Heath is personally involved in the negotiations because he believes membership will promote peace and stability between Britain and Europe.

1 January 1973 - Britain joins the Common Market

1973-1975 world recession hits hard

The booming 1960s comes to an end as a world recession hits, exasperated by the 1973 oil crisis. The Organization of Arab Petroleum Exporting Countries (OPEC) places an embargo on nations they think are supporting Israel during the Yom Kippur War (6-26 October 1973). The embargo initially targets Britain, the United States, Canada, Japan, and the Netherlands. By the end of the embargo in March 1974, the price of oil has risen nearly 400%, from $3 per barrel to nearly $12. Inflation peaks at 20%. A three-day working week is introduced in January 1974 as electricity is rationed due to fears of a power shortage as a result of a bitter miners' strike. They demand a 35% pay rise and reject an offer of a 16% pay increase. Edward Heath calls a snap election on 28 February 1974 and loses.

France is hit very hard by a severe currency shortage. They take the unusual step of limiting imports by only allowing goods in through one port. This causes chaos. Complaints are made that the move contravenes EEC rules with regard to the free movement of goods.

February 1974 - Labour's minority government

Opinion polls give the Tories a comfortable win and get it wrong - again. Labour wins four seats more than the Conservatives. This results in a hung parliament.

Labour with 17 seats short of a majority refuses to form a coalition with Ted Heath, who then resigns.

Heath's resignation allows the MP for Finchley, Margaret Thatcher, to become leader of the Opposition.

Wilson gives the miners a 29% wage rise to gain time to put his energy policy in place, which will result in mass closures.

As leader of the Labour Party Harold Wilson gives an interview on his winning manifesto and issues of the day. Right at the beginning he says: 'On food prices, apart from renegotiating the terms of entry into the Common Market, we will have strict price control ... We shall have food subsidies on the most important items in the housewife's family budget.' These are measures required to counteract the food price hike that resulted from implementing the CAP after joining the EEC a year earlier.

↳ brexitchronicles.co.uk/mc/HW

October 1974 - Elections give Labour a clear majority

As expected, PM Harold Wilson calls another election after finding it impossible to form a stable government. Labour wins 319 seats and beats Margaret Thatcher's Conservative Party, but has a majority of just one seat in the House.

Labour fought the election on a commitment to renegotiate the terms of EEC membership and to hold a referendum on whether to remain on renegotiated terms or to leave.

This is the same tactic used by PM David Cameron as the basis for the 2016 referendum.

MP Enoch Powell (b. 1912, d. 1998), an outspoken Eurosceptic, leaves the Conservatives after denouncing Margaret Thatcher's policies on the Common Market. He wins the seat for South Down as one of only 12 members of the Ulster Unionist Party (which governed Northern Ireland 1921–1972).

May 1975 - Television plays an important role

There is a heated television debate on the forthcoming referendum between the former Conservative Prime Minister Edward Heath (pro-Europe) and Labour MP Michael Foot (Eurosceptic).

   brexitchronicles.co.uk/RD

June 1975 - The first in-out referendum

The country is now under a Labour government led by Harold Wilson. The Labour party is bitterly divided on Europe. The Labour manifesto calls for an in-out referendum to allow people the opportunity to decide whether Britain should stay in the Common Market on renegotiated terms or whether it should leave. The referendum happens on 5 June 1975.

The renegotiation of terms revolves around payments to the CAP. Harold Wilson achieves some reductions to British payments, but the amount is minimal and the issue is still there. New Zealand is allowed market access for their dairy products. The European Regional Development Fund (ERDF) is created to help farmers in Britain's poorer regions. It is agreed that a 'corrective mechanism' that would apply to all countries in economic difficulties will be set up in May 1976. Britain will never benefit from the ERDF as the discovery of North Sea oil means Britain will contribute 20% of Community revenue but only receive 12% of its expenditure.

In hindsight, not what you would call a fantastic deal.

Harold Wilson runs a campaign to support remaining in the Community. He promotes the negotiated terms as a huge success. The new Leader of the Opposition, Margaret Thatcher, supports him.

An interview in May 1975 with Labour Prime Minister Harold Wilson, who is riding a political high at the time, discusses the implications of the forthcoming referendum on 6 June 1975.

↰ brexitchronicles.co.uk/RI

As a leader supposedly promoting a vote to remain, it is interesting how important the Commonwealth is to Wilson - who has just returned from a two-week Commonwealth conference. He says, 'Remember, I have never been an emotional European... I am an emotional Commonwealth man.'

He goes on to say that it would certainly be a traumatic experience should Britain leave the EEC because a lot has happened in the last three years. He claims that Britain has been able to make changes to the agreement with the EEC.

Later on in the interview Wilson explains how the referendum has polarized the nation and Parliament.

Q: 'Mr Eric Deacon, Undersecretary at the Department of Trade, said that most major foodstuffs are costing Britain more than if we were outside the EEC. Is that true?'

Wilson gets flustered and attempts to deflect, then says: 'The food issue is a very important one and a difficult one, it is a fact that certainly we have not had to pay more for food as a result of being in the Market. Others might say that it's been a period of temporary higher prices. I am satisfied that we certainly couldn't have got our food cheaper anywhere else.'

He also mentions the butter and beef mountains caused by an over-production that was a direct result of the CAP.

Here is leader and instigator of the No campaign, Labour MP Tony Benn, in action. The campaign against Benn, by a press who supported remaining, was vicious. He is tipped to be prime minister one day, which Wilson puts a stop to in subsequent years.

↳ brexitchronicles.co.uk/mc/TB

The title of one pamphlet for the No campaign says: THE RIGHT TO RULE OURSELVES. The fundamental question is whether or not we remain free to rule ourselves in our own way.

Tony Benn (Lab) and Roy Jenkins (Lab, President of the European Commission 1977-1981) debate the referendum.

↳ brexitchronicles.co.uk/cm/RJ

> **Referendum results: 67.23% remain; 32.77% leave**

March 1976 - Harold Wilson resigns as Prime Minister

The recession had been officially declared over in 1975 but unemployment is the highest ever, topping the one million mark, strikes cripple the manufacturing and public service sectors, and inflation remains very high. Harold Wilson resigns.

His successor, James Callaghan, takes a multibillion-pound bail-out from the International Monetary Fund (IMF) to bolster Britain's wavering economy. He attempts to negotiate British contributions to Brussels yet again, but to no avail.

December 1976 - MP Enoch Powell makes a speech to Parliament with some accurate predictions about the EEC.

↳ brexitchronicles.co.uk/mc/EP

March 1979 - Exchange rate mechanism created

The exchange rate mechanism (ERM) is launched to stabilize exchange rates across the EEC. This is a precursor to introducing a single currency.

It means that participants are obliged to keep their exchange rates within 2.25% on either side of a given exchange rate. It is pegged to the Deutschmark, which makes sense since Germany has the biggest and most stable economy in Europe.

The Labour Chancellor of the Exchequer, MP Denis Healey (1974–1979, famous for his bushy eyebrows), is deeply concerned that, by tying EEC currencies to the Deutschmark, the ERM will benefit the German economy at the expense of other member countries.

All EEC states take part from day one - except Britain

The issue of Britain joining the ERM is discussed in Parliament no fewer than eight times between 1979 and 1990. After which a reluctant prime minister agrees to join, under pressure.

Just two years on Britain is forced to exit the ERM as Germany increases interest rates and requests that Britain devalue the pound. Denis Healey had predicted this danger ten years earlier. Britain pays a heavy price and never re-joins the exchange rate mechanism.

CHAPTER THREE

The Thatcher Years

The very mention of her name stirs passion in anyone who lived through the Thatcher years. People either admire her or hate her. She is one of the most influential politicians in the European building process. Her actions and ideas change the face of EEC-British relations like no other leader.

Margaret Thatcher is a champion of the Eurosceptics, a defender of national sovereignty, and of the independence of EEC member states from European institutions.

Always conscious of the benefits to be derived from membership of the Common Market she has no intention of destroying the European building process. She just wants to redirect it from supranational aspirations to national cooperation.

Margaret Hilda Roberts is born in October 1925, in Grantham, a small town in Lincolnshire, England. Her father, Alfred Roberts, owns two grocery stores, is an active member of the local council, and is a Methodist preacher. He is also Mayor of Grantham for two years just after World War II.

Margaret Roberts wins a scholarship to study chemistry at Oxford University (1943-1947). Even then she shows an interest in politics and becomes President of the Oxford University Conservative Association in 1946.

Two years later she joins the local Conservative Association and attends her first party conference in Llandudno, Wales. At the tender age of just 24 she is asked to become the Conservative candidate for Dartford (a safe Labour seat) in February 1949. At the celebratory dinner for winning the candidacy she meets Denis Thatcher. They get married three years later.

As a candidate for Dartford it makes sense to move there. She supports herself as a research chemist. She loses two elections (1950 and 1951) but nevertheless reduces the Labour majority by 7,000.

It takes ten years for her to claim a seat in Parliament, as MP for Finchley in October 1959.

Thirty years after standing for Dartford she becomes the longest-serving British Prime Minister of the 20th century.

May 1979 - Conservatives win election

Thatcher tables and wins a vote of no confidence. This forces Labour PM Jim Callaghan to call an election. The country is still reeling from the 'winter of discontent' with high inflation (17%), drawn-out strikes, and unemployment at 1.56 million. All this damages Labour's standing in the polls. The Conservatives gain 62 seats, Labour loses 50. The SNP, with 71 candidates, only wins two seats.

The Conservatives take back power with Margaret Thatcher, the first female Prime Minister, at the helm.

She arrives at 10 Downing Street for the first time and gives a short interview that mentions the assassination (car bomb) of MP Mr Airey Neave her campaign manager.

↳   brexitchronicles.co.uk/cm/MT

The incoming government inherits a country in trouble and bankrupt. The problems it needs to solve include tackling inflation, reducing the national debt, which is 44.5% of GDP, and getting the trade unions in line.

Although Britain is the third-poorest country in the EEC (Germany and France are richer) it is nevertheless required to make a net contribution to EEC coffers of £1 billion per year (equivalent to £10 billion in 2019), which is far more than other countries but in return for less.

Thatcher goes about the task of sorting out Britain's finances by raising interest rates to 17% and cutting public spending. This isn't popular as it causes unemployment to double to three million within five years. A deep recession ensues.

Thatcher decides to sell off council houses to raise money - many council estates are run down and the cost of maintenance outweighs the income from rents. The Right to Buy policy comes into force in 1980. In 1981, 66,321 purchases are made and 174,697 in 1982. The sales bring in £692 million in 1980/1, £1.4 billion in 1981/2 and £1.98 billion in 1982/3. This helps put fiscal Britain back on track.

An oversupply of milk products in the marketplace hits the news again - dubbed 'the butter mountain'.

Declassified documents published by the National Archives give an insight to how Mrs Thatcher feels about the Common Fisheries Policy. In September 1979 she notes:

'The fisheries situation was already sufficiently unsatisfactory without our making further concessions. The so-called reciprocity of historic sights was meaningless since the French had fished out their own waters and British access to those waters was worthless.'

June 1983 - Thatcher elected for second term

A crippling defeat of a Labour Party led by Michael Foot. For the previous three years their manifesto had called for Britain to withdraw from the EEC without a referendum.

Conservatives have 397 seats, Labour has 209. This is the largest parliamentary majority of the post-war era. Thatcher is on a roll and Thatcherism is the new buzz word. She now has a mandate to radically change a nation.

No fewer than three future Labour Party leaders take their seats in Parliament for the first time: Tony Blair (Lab), MP for Sedgefield; Gordon Brown (Con), MP for Dunfermline East; and Jeremy Corbyn (Lab), MP for Islington North.

June 1984 - 66% British rebate agreed

Margaret Thatcher successfully negotiates a multibillion pound rebate of 66%, to be given back to Britain from EEC contributions. A summary from decision makers of the day.

↳ brexitchronicles.co.uk/mc/BG

Lord Owens comment, 'The arithmetic was really bad for Britain', sums up the true situation in the country, created by the CAP.

1984-1985 Miners' strike

A once-proud, nationalized mining industry becomes unprofitable as a result of alternative energy, such as nuclear power, North Sea natural gas, and cheaper coal from abroad. Pit closures are inevitable.

Arthur Scargill leads 187,000 mineworkers, angry about mass pit closures that follow the government's withdrawal of subsidies. But the National Union of Miners (NUM) fails to hold a ballot of its members, so the strike is ruled illegal in September 1984. However, it continues to 3 March 1985. The government wins and by 2009 only six working pits remain in the UK, compared to 174 in 1983.

What makes this strike so memorable is the strength of emotions and the violence against those workers who won't strike. Strike breakers are called scabs and strike supporters, called flying pickets, are bussed to producing collieries. Over 12 months' six people die and 11,300 are arrested. This footage shows pickets and police clashing at Orgreave Colliery.

↳ brexitchronicles.co.uk/mc/MS

October 1984 - IRA Brighton bombing

↳ brexitchronicles.co.uk/cm/BB

January 1985 - How people see the EEC

The bumpy road to British-EEC harmonization is highlighted by this fantastic debate between two MEPs, David Curry (Con) and Bob Cryer (Lab, a Eurosceptic), and a very well informed pro-European, Kenneth Williams (of Carry On fame) in front of a highly emotional European and British audience.

The issues and opinions expressed in 1985 don't differ from the concerns and prejudices people have in 2016. MEP Bob Cryer's talk of reform, and some of the opinions expressed, demonstrate how long this discussion has been going on for. It's always a pleasure to watch Kenneth Williams.

   brexitchronicles.co.uk/mc/KW

June 1985 - Schengen Treaty signed

The Treaty is an agreement to get rid of controls at common borders. It is signed near the small town of Schengen in Luxembourg. There is a lack of consensus among members and only five of the ten member states are signatories: France, West Germany, Belgium, Luxembourg, and the Netherlands. Britain doesn't sign up and opts out completely, as does Ireland.

Schengen becomes a core part of EU law in 1999, so all members are legally obliged to sign up for it. The UK and Ireland retain their option to opt out.

February 1985 - Greenland leaves EEC

Greenland is granted home rule in 1979 by Denmark and holds an in-out referendum in February 1982 - 53% vote to leave the EEC. The result is hardly surprising as 70% voted against joining in 1972; but they were then a county of Denmark, where 63% were for join.

Grøxit, that's not something you say after someone sneezes, it's their version of Brexit. This is the first time a territory votes to leave the EEC. Their main gripe is with the Common Fisheries Policy and control over Greenland's fish resources, especially shrimps and prawns. Other countries are fishing in their waters and depleting stocks.

The ensuing Treaty refers to Greenland as a 'special case' with regard to its supranational European affiliation and the country is later granted OCT-status.

Overseas Countries and Territories Association (OCT)

This Association, founded in 2000, promotes the economic and social development of the OCTs and their close economic relations with the Community. The EU grants unilateral trade preferences (duty-free quota-free access to the EU) to all products originating in the OCTs. The rules of origin stipulate the conditions under which this preferential access is to be enjoyed by the beneficiary countries. You could say it's cherry picking.

February 1986 - Single European Act signed

To launch an ambitious plan to create a single market, the Single European Act (SEA) comes into force on 1 July 1987 as a precursor to the European Community (EC). This is the first major revision of the 1957 Treaty of Rome. It gives legislative powers to the European Parliament for the first time and heralds the free movement of goods, capital, labour, and services known as 'the four freedoms'.

It is ratified by the British Parliament, without consulting the British people. After signing this treaty Thatcher becomes sceptical of the overall EEC project because of policies that are leading to monetary union.

The Danish parliament rejects it, believing the Act gives too much power to the European Parliament. But a Danish national referendum, held in February 1986, approves the Treaty.

The Italians delay signing it for the opposite reason, that it doesn't give enough powers to the European Parliament.

The Irish hold a referendum in May 1987 because signing it requires a change in their constitution - 69.9% vote in favour, with a turnout of just 44.1%.

Spain, Portugal and Greece emerge from dictatorships in the 1970s. A 'democratic' Greece joined the EEC in January 1981, followed by Spain and Portugal in 1986. The northern Mediterranean is now part of the EEC.

June 1987 - Thatcher elected for third term

There's a notable rise in people's living standards due to the policies of the previous two terms. Inflation is only 4%, (lowest level in 20 years), there is a strong economy, and lower taxes. A landslide victory for the Conservative Party (376 seats to Labour's 229) is hardly surprising.

Margaret Thatcher becomes the first prime minister in 160 years to win three successive terms in office. She has earned the title of Iron Lady and continues with the ideology named after her, Thatcherism.

Both former Labour Prime Minister James Callaghan and MP Enoch Powell lose their seats, never to return to politics.

Alex Salmond (SNP) arrives on the scene. He wins the seat for Banff and Buchan with 44.3% of the votes. Just three years later he becomes leader of the Scottish National Party and a First Minister of Scotland (2007-2014).

September 1988 - Thatcher's Bruges speech

On 21 September 1988 Margaret Thatcher delivers a speech about her vision for future relationships between Britain and Europe. This is her response to the first draft of what was to become known as the Maastricht Treaty. She is concerned about a power grab by the European Commission. The speech is her attempt to persuade EEC policy makers to change course.

It's a clear message to the attending senior EEC officials that she will oppose any attempt to turn the EEC into an economic and political union. She lays down five guiding principles. Here are some excerpts from the speech.

↳ brexitchronicles.co.uk/cm/BT

Thatcher's five guiding principles

1. Willing cooperation between sovereign states

'My first guiding principle is this: willing and active cooperation between independent sovereign states is the best way to build a successful European Community.'

The operative words here are willing and independent sovereign states - in other words, not becoming a United States of Europe. She went on to say:

'Europe will be stronger precisely because it has France as France, Spain as Spain, Britain as Britain, each with its own customs, traditions and identity. It would be folly to try to fit them into some sort of identikit European personality.'

2. Encouraging change

'My second guiding principle is this: Community policies must tackle present problems in a practical way, however difficult that may be.'

'If we cannot reform those Community policies which are patently wrong (referring to CAP) or ineffective and which are rightly causing public disquiet, then we shall not get the public support for the Community's future development.'

'It was not right that half the total Community budget was being spent on storing and disposing of surplus food (referring to the butter mountain caused by CAP) ... Now those stocks are being sharply reduced (price dumping due to a surplus, which ruins the livelihoods of British farmers).'

3. Europe open to enterprise

'My third guiding principle is the need for Community policies which encourage enterprise.'

'That a state-controlled economy is a recipe for low growth and that free enterprise within a framework of law brings better results.'

'Of course, we must make it easier for people to travel throughout the Community. But it is a matter of plain common sense that we cannot totally abolish frontier controls if we are also to protect our citizens from crime and stop the movement of drugs, of terrorists and of illegal immigrants.'

4. Europe open to the world

'My fourth guiding principle is that Europe should not be protectionist.'

5. Europe and defence

'My last guiding principle concerns the most fundamental issue - the European countries' role in defence. Europe must continue to maintain a sure defence through NATO.'

'But let us never forget that our way of life, our vision and all we hope to achieve, is secured not by the rightness of our cause but by the strength of our defence.'

'On this, we must never falter, never fail.'

Summing up the British approach

'Mr Chairman, I believe it is not enough just to talk in general terms about a European vision or ideal. If we believe in it, we must chart the way ahead and identify the next steps. And that is what I have tried to do this evening.'

1988 - EEC regional aid doubled

Market liberalization helped northern European members to become richer. Poorer southern states, such as Greece (joining 1981), Spain, and Portugal (joining 1986) demand compensation. This comes in the form of a cohesion policy through which thousands of projects receive huge financial support from structural funds. The money helps to construct roads, bridges, factories, airports - to aid regional development.

October 1990 - Britain becomes party to the ERM

Britain joins the exchange rate mechanism 11 years after it is created to stabilize exchange rates within the EEC.

The growth and scale of export/import businesses is moving into the billions of pounds each year. This requires a stable rate of exchange so that you know how much you will be getting or paying for goods or services when dealing with other countries.

With the pound floating freely against all other currencies, businesses could not be sure how much they would be paying for something in the future. A fluctuating exchange rate can cause a price to be significantly higher or lower.

During the 1980s there are heated discussions between the then Chancellor of the Exchequer, Nigel Lawson, and Margaret Thatcher, who is against ERM. Lawson resigns in 1989. He is replaced by John Major, who now persuades Thatcher to join.

Politicians are enthusiastic, they believe it will help lower inflation and move Britain closer to European integration, giving it more influence. The effect of Britain joining the ERM is immediate: interest rates drop for the first time in a year; there is a massive rise in share prices; the value of the pound increases.

The interest rate is the tool available to governments to ensure that their currency stays within ERM bandwidths.

November 1990 - Thatcher ousted as PM

Two years after giving her Bruges speech she is in Parliament condemning Europe's approach to building a union in her famous 'no, no, no' speech on 30 October 1990. She isn't hiding her hostility toward Europe and upsets her pro-Europe government, which eventually leads to her downfall.

Here is that speech. Watch Douglas Hurd sitting directly to her left, he is the one who later signs the Maastricht Treaty.

↳ brexitchronicles.co.uk/mc/NO

The Conservative party, bullied by Thatcher for so many years, is not happy and is about to revolt. The Deputy Chief Whip, Lord Garel-Jones, had warned Thatcher a year earlier to soften her anti-European rhetoric and had asked her to reconsider her highly unpopular flagship policy (community charge or poll tax) to help improve MPs' re-election chances. He says, 'There are a hundred assassins lurking in the bushes and in a year's time they are going to come out and kill you!' How right he is.

Her popularity takes a hit as the economy takes a downturn, inflation rises, and interest rates increase. A chain of events - triggered by the resignation of Deputy Prime Minister Sir Geoffrey Howe two days after Thatcher's 'no, no, no' speech - goes down as the biggest betrayal of any leader in British history.

1 November 1990 - Sir Geoffrey Howe resigns

In a Cabinet reshuffle in July 1989 Sir Geoffrey Howe is sacked as Foreign Secretary and replaced by John Major. This also means he has to give up the Foreign Secretary's country residence, Chevening, a luxury 15-bedroom mansion in Kent.

Howe is appointed Leader of the House of Commons, Lord President of the Council and Deputy Prime Minister. You might think this is a promotion, it isn't.

Howe resigns on 1 November 1990, just two days after Thatcher's 'no, no, no' speech.

Sir Geoffrey Howe, who believes deeply in European unity, gives a scathing resignation speech criticizing Thatcher's resolve to stop further EEC integration. He points out how different the relationship might have been if Britain had signed the Treaty of Rome in 1957, which would have given Britain more control from the onset.

↳ brexitchronicles.co.uk/cm/GH

This resignation speech triggers a series of events that happen at breakneck speed and that lead to a head-to-head leadership competition, which Thatcher believes she can easily win.

Howe gives up being an MP at the April 1992 general election and is made a life peer in June that year, which gives him a seat in the House of Lords. He retires in May 2015.

Heseltine's leadership bid

Thatcher hears that Michael Heseltine is drumming up support for a leadership contest. She confronts him with an ultimatum, 'put up or shut up' - a war cry John Major uses some years later when faced with a similar challenge.

Confident she will win a leadership challenge, she brings forward the election contest date to 20 November 1990. She wants to get it over with quickly to limit any damage it may do to the party.

Heseltine, spurred on by Howe's resignation speech the day before, picks up the gauntlet on 14 November and announces his intention to stand against Thatcher in a leadership election.

Round one - Let the contest begin

The Conservative Party leadership election is to take place on 20 November 1990. There are only six days to prepare. The race is on.

Thatcher agrees not to campaign personally; she avoids television and radio. She only gives two press interviews, in both of which, when the issue of a single currency is raised, she says firmly that she is prepared to put the issue to the people.

As her party is deciding her fate she keeps to a busy schedule as PM: visits troops in Northern Ireland on 16 November; attends the European Summit in Paris from 19-21 November, hobnobs with world leaders and signs the Paris Charter. She wants to give an impression of confidence and is still in Paris on the day voting takes place.

Lord Heseltine is a serious contender. A millionaire by 35 and a Cabinet member at 41, he'd never thought Margaret Thatcher was leadership material and couldn't understand how she'd got the votes in 1974. He is contemptuous of her working-class background.

His last Cabinet post was as Defence Secretary (1983-1986). A scandal involving Westland helicopters - leaked letters and a desire to keep them British or bust - forces him to resign. In his resignation speech he refers to Thatcher as a liar who lacks integrity. He becomes a backbencher in 1986. He still hankers for the crown and this is his one and only chance to get it.

↳   brexitchronicles.co.uk/mc/TS

Although Thatcher defeats Heseltine by 204 to 152 votes from Tory MPs she doesn't win. Parliamentary rules require that the winner gets 15% more votes than their opponent. The margin of her victory is just four votes short of the 15% rule. A second election must be called.

She consults with her Cabinet, then withdraws from the race. This surely makes Heseltine the natural winner. MP Cecil Parkinson says, 'She stepped aside to let John Major or Douglas Hurd win.'

Round Two - The more the merrier

The Cabinet don't want Heseltine (a backbencher) as PM and decide only a Cabinet member should succeed. They allow two new contenders to enter the race, blocking Heseltine from being pronounced winner and forcing a second election on 27 November 1990. The line-up is:

Michael Heseltine	Pro-Europe
Douglas Hurd	Pro-Europe (signs Maastricht Treaty)
John Major	Pro-Europe (signs Maastricht Treaty)

Thatcher lobbies hard in support of John Major, who receives most votes (49.7%), still two votes short of the 15% rule. As the result is announced Heseltine and Hurd withdraw their candidacies. The most unlikely candidate with the least experience wins. Enter John Major. A news report explains how Heseltine's bid is sabotaged.

  brexitchronicles.co.uk/mc/MH

In Thatcher's last speech in the House of Commons on 22 November 1990, she is still fighting the cause as she says to Labour Opposition Leader Neil Kinnock, 'On the central issues of Europe's future they will not tell us where they stand. Do they want a single currency? The Right Honourable Gentleman doesn't even know what it means ...'

brexitchronicles.co.uk/cm/LS

Final twist to a sorry tale

On the morning of 22 November 1990, Thatcher announces her decision to stand down as Prime Minister. That afternoon, Labour table a vote of no confidence which, curiously, she wins with an overwhelming vote of confidence. Had she lost this vote it might have triggered a general election.

BRIEF TIMELINE

30 October 1990 - Thatcher gives her 'no, no, no' speech

1 November 1990 - Sir Geoffrey Howe resigns

14 November 1990 - Michael Heseltine's leadership bid

20 November 1990 - First round of leadership elections

22 November 1990 - Thatcher concedes defeat and resigns

27 November 1990 - Second round of leadership elections -
as his two opponents withdraw,
John Major is elected.

After being deposed Margaret Thatcher continues as a backbencher MP and is not silenced on the issue of the EU.

The question in my mind is whether she would have created a different dynamic in today's Britain if she'd not been ousted by a handful of her party. In my opinion, her negotiating skills would have given Britain a better position within Europe.

Thatcher gives up her seat in the Commons just before the 1992 general elections. She becomes a member of the House of Lords in the same year and makes a series of speeches criticizing the Maastricht Treaty, describing it as 'a treaty too far' and states: 'I could never have signed this treaty.'

In 2003 Thatcher publishes Statecraft, in which she says that Britain should leave the Common Market.

February 1991 - Assassination attempt on John Major

↳ brexitchronicles.co.uk/cm/JM

November 1991 - UKIP created

Alan Sked MP, a Eurosceptic who believes the EEC is corrupt and anti-democratic, and is a risk to the British economy, forms the Anti-Federalist League (AFL) in London. It is renamed the UK Independence Party (UKIP) in September 1993.

A touch of nostalgia for those who were there.

↳ brexitchronicles.co.uk/mc/PA

BOOK TWO

THE POST-THATCHER YEARS

(1992 - 2016)

INTRODUCTION

Lest We Forget

Margaret Thatcher had fought hard for Britain's position in Europe, trying to outwit countries that had set up an institution designed to work in their own interests, which are not necessarily Britain's.

Like a Shakespearean tragedy she is dethroned in an unceremonious manner by those closest to her. The conspirators persuade Thatcher's Foreign Secretary, Sir Geoffrey Howe, to lead the plot to stop her from scuppering the EU master plan. Lord Heseltine seizes his chance to be king but fails to take the throne by losing the joust to the grey knave.

Well, maybe not quite so dramatic - but Britain is now in a post-Thatcher era.

The tabling of the most comprehensive and far-reaching treaty the EEC had ever constructed is about to be thrust upon a very willing new leader. The annexation of Britain by the EU is in full swing and is given the green light by parliament. Yet again, the Government of the day, led by John Major, doesn't see the need to consult the British people about a Treaty of such magnitude.

John Major was born and raised in the south of England, his first job was working for an insurance broker. He couldn't find a decent job so took a correspondence course in banking, which got him a job in a bank in 1965. In 1959, aged 16, he joined the Young Conservatives in Brixton. In 1964 he stood as a candidate for Lambeth Borough Council, and was elected as a councillor in 1968. Up until 1971 he was Chairman of the Housing Committee, overseeing several housing estate developments in Lambeth.

Major's first attempt to stand for parliament is for St. Pancras North in the February and October 1974 elections – he is defeated on both occasions. In May 1979 he is selected for the safe Conservative seat of Huntingdon and enters parliament for the first time - along with Thatcher becoming Prime Minister.

After two years as an MP he's appointed as a parliamentary private secretary then to assistant whip in 1983, Under Secretary of State for Social Security in 1985, then Minister of State for the same department a year later.

John Major is offered his first Cabinet position after retaining his seat in the 1987 elections. Just ten years after becoming an MP Thatcher offers him Geoffrey Howe's job as Foreign Secretary then appoints him as Chancellor of the Exchequer just three months later, in October 1989 (that correspondence course in banking must have sealed the deal). In the space of two years he's gone from junior minister to two top Cabinet positions.

CHAPTER FOUR

THE MAJOR ERRORS

December 1991 - Signing draft Maastricht Treaty

A country in recession and with rising unemployment now has a less than charismatic prime minister at the helm (compared to his predecessor). John Major has a lot on his plate.

Major's claim to power on 27 November 1990 is the pinnacle of a whirlwind career spanning three years. He is not leader through a democratic process and the support of the British electorate, but through a Conservative Party vote to replace the increasingly Eurosceptic Margaret Thatcher - who would never have signed the Maastricht Treaty. She's a tough act to follow. Major, as a pro-Europe supporter, is about to negotiate a new membership that will take Britain to the next level.

John Major sees no reason to call a referendum to ratify the Maastricht Treaty, despite calls from his party, and a bill passes through parliament with only 17 votes in favour. On 11 December 1991, just 12 months after taking office, John Major signs the draft Maastricht Treaty (MT) that turns the EEC into the EU. 'Game, set and match for Britain,' he is supposed to have said.

↳ brexitchronicles.co.uk/ce/TM

The irony is that some 28 years later, in 2019, the very same John Major is fighting the case for a second referendum - when he hadn't even offered an unsuspecting public one referendum before signing that treaty.

THE CRUX OF IT

No referendum to join but let's have two referendums if you want to leave.

The Maastricht Treaty, among other things, paves the way for monetary union and includes a chapter on social policy (workers' rights). Major negotiates an opt-out on both issues. In parliament, Labour and Liberal Democrats oppose the opt-out to the social policy but to no avail. The treaty also introduces European citizenship that gives Europeans the right to live and work, and to vote in elections, in any EU country.

A brief guide to the Maastricht Treaty

The then president of France, Francois Mitterrand (1981-1995) and the German chancellor, Dr. Helmut Kohl (1982-1988) who receives the title 'Honorary citizen of Europe' in December 1998, are both instrumental in the creation of the Maastricht Treaty. Kohl's life's work revolves around the unification of Germany, the improvement of cooperation between European countries, and the creation of an economic and monetary union. In short, his vision is a politically integrated Europe. Realizing this gives Germany the means of achieving a second German industrial miracle - it had enjoyed the first just after World War II.

As with every previous EEC treaty the Maastricht Treaty is constructed mainly by Germany and France. It replaces or amends all previous treaties and changes the 'community' into a 'union' based on three pillars, or policies.

1. The Single European Act

This is really an extension of the Single European Act (SEA) agreed in February 1986. No duties on imports/exports and no borders. One of the biggest changes is that the European Parliament now gains more powers over member states.

2. A common foreign and security policy

This is probably one of the most difficult parts for member states to deal with. For example, after Yugoslavia split in 1990, member states could not agree on whether to recognize the newly created states; neither could they decide where to relocate migrants entering via Italy or Greece.

3. Cooperation on justice and home affairs

This covers things like, judicial cooperation in criminal and civil matters; the creation of a European Police Office (Europol); and combating terrorism, serious crime, drug trafficking, and international fraud.

In real terms this signals an intention to:

1. establish a European Union with no internal borders

2. lay the foundations for a single currency (euro)

3. create a common citizenship - the EU Passport

4. give greater euro-parliamentary powers to Brussels

5. create a common foreign and defence policy

6. promote closer cooperation to fight crime

7. introduce a central banking system

April 1992 - Conservatives win election

Here is the news, four days before the general election.

 brexitchronicles.co.uk/ec/CG

The Conservatives led by John Major retain control of the Government for a fourth consecutive term, against all the odds. They win by 336 seats to Labour's 271 – the opinion polls had favoured Labour leader Neil Kinnock.

The country goes deeper into recession - Major is not going to have an easy tenure. Five months into his term a decision that he had advised Thatcher to take on board explodes.

September 1992 - Black Wednesday, a sorry ERM tale

Britain joined the Exchange Rate Mechanism (ERM) when the country was on the verge of a recession and the pound was overvalued by around 10%.

Uncertainty over Danish and French referendums is just one of the causes of the turmoil affecting the currency markets. International currency speculators begin to sell off the pound, devaluing it below the mandatary limits set out by the ERM. Attempts to prop it up cost the Government an estimated £3 billion from Britain's reserves and force a rise in interest rates to 15%. The pound is suspended from the ERM on 16 September 1992, never to return.

 brexitchronicles.co.uk/ce/BW

Ratification by all Members

Remember that peculiarity of a treaty being signed first then ratification being sought? This is no different.

After John Major signs the draft Maastricht Treaty in December 1991 he then goes back to Parliament for ratification.

Out of the 12 countries who sign the draft treaty in December 1991, only four hold a referendum, as required by their respective constitutions:

Italy (advisory) on May 1989 - 88.1% in favour

Ireland on 18 June 1992 - 69.1% in favour

France on 20 September 1992 - 50.8% in favour

Denmark on 2 June 1992 - rejected by 50.7%.

Denmark rejects the treaty

The treaty can only come into effect if all 12 member states ratify it. The rejection from Denmark poses a real threat to the project and has to be resolved quickly. Denmark successfully negotiates opt-outs on the single currency, defence integration, citizenship rights and home affairs. These amendments are called the Edinburgh Agreement.

Denmark holds a second referendum on 18 May 1993 on the basis of the four opt-outs outlined above - 56.7% vote in favour.

The British Parliament is not obliged to seek approval by referendum as they have the doctrine of parliamentary sovereignty with legislative powers. This means they hold a debate, then vote for or against the issue.

Parliament decides on treaty implementation

The draft treaty outlining the agreement was passed by Parliament in December 1991 by only 17 votes.

It is now up to John Major to get full parliamentary approval to the Maastricht Treaty through a series of votes and amendments in the House of Commons. It was never going to be easy as the Conservatives only have an 18-seat majority, meaning that every vote counts.

Enter the Maastricht Rebels

The Conservative Eurosceptic faction is growing in numbers and lobbying hard against the treaty. They even risk having the whip withdrawn by voting with the Opposition and against their own Government to defeat bills. They also draw up some 400 amendments to the treaty and have some success in getting them implemented. Labour also tables lots of amendments in an attempt to align it to their social and economic policies.

The Maastricht Rebels insist that if a referendum is held, they will stop trying to block the treaty. A referendum is repeatedly ruled out by John Major's Government.

On the really big issues that the rebels oppose - like opting out of the 'Social Chapter' that covers workers' pay, health, and safety - they're unable to wield any influence.

↳ brexitchronicles.co.uk/ec/MR

There are 20-plus core Maastricht Rebels - one is Margaret Thatcher, who has stayed on as a backbench MP after her ousting. With a House majority of only 18 seats this gives the rebels immense power when it comes to a vote.

These are some of the rebels who go on to prominent positions within Government in later years:

Alan Duncan, Liam Fox, John Biffen, Bill Walker, Michael Spicer, Peter Tapsell, Andrew Hunter, George Gardiner, Barry Legg.

Bill Cash, Roger Knapman, Christopher Gill, Teresa Gorman and Richard Body went on to join UKIP.

In May 2016 Iain Duncan Smith is asked about voting against Maastricht.

⤷ brexitchronicles.co.uk/ec/DS

One of the rebels' first successes is in March 1993. They vote against their own party and pass an amendment by 22 votes to ensure that anybody sitting on any European Community committee has to be a duly elected representative.

This amendment has not avoided such situations as that highlighted by Nigel Farage MEP on 24 February 2010, that the first permanent President of the EU Council, Mr Herman Van Rompuy (2009-2014), had not been duly elected to the position.

⤷ brexitchronicles.co.uk/NF

July 1993 - Maastricht end game

Ratification of the Maastricht Treaty (MT) comes to a head. There is a final stumbling block, which is resolved with a brilliant trick: make acceptance of the bill a question of confidence in the Government. If the bill now fails it will trigger an election, which risks the Conservatives losing power as they're popularity wanes.

On 6 May Liberal Democrats win a Conservative safe seat in the Newbury by-election with a massive swing of 28.4%.

The Labour opposition tables an amendment on 22 July 1993 to postpone incorporation of the Treaty until the Government adopts the Social Chapter. The result is a tie - Ayes 317, Noes 317. The Speaker of the House has the casting vote, which he gives to the Government. The bill fails allowing the treaty to progress. The Government then loses their main motion in the Maastricht ratification debate as MPs block it by 324 to 316.

The next day, 23 July 1993, John Major tables an emergency confidence motion, worded as follows:

> *'This House has confidence in the policy of the Government on the adoption of the protocol on social policy.'*

Instead of a vote for the bill it becomes a vote of confidence in the Government. MPs feel held to ransom over a bill they're not in favour of. Government wins by 40 votes. All the rebels vote for the bill, only MP Rupert Allason (Con) abstains, the whip is withdrawn as punishment.

Why the Social Chapter is a deal breaker?

The opt-out to the Social Chapter negotiated by John Major is one of the main issues of concern to the Maastricht Rebels. The Labour and Liberal Democrat leaders also feel strongly that anything to do with the protection of workers' rights should be included in the treaty.

The Tory Government feels it would cost companies too much to implement and since they'd already successfully negotiated the opt-out with Brussels they just required ratification by Parliament.

In May 1997 Labour's Foreign Secretary, Robin Cook, finally signs up to just two directives within the Social Chapter:

1. The Works Council directive, which requires employers to consult employees before making major changes in the workplace

2. The Parental Leave directive, which specifies that parents should be allowed a maximum of three months unpaid leave after the birth of a child, to be taken over eight years.

July 1993 - legal action to stop Parliament ratifying MT

Lord Rees-Mogg (father of Jacob Rees-Mogg MP, Con) launches a legal action a week after the bill is passed by the Commons in an attempt to stop Major's Government ratifying the Maastricht Treaty. The High Court rule in favour of Government on all three counts, which removes the last obstacle to ratification.

The Conservatives are beginning to lose seats in by-elections. On 29 July 1993 the constituency of Christchurch, a Conservative safe seat with a majority of 23,000, goes to the Liberal Democrats with a majority of 16,000.

November 1993 - Maastricht Treaty in force

From its signing in February 1992 it only took 21 months for 12 countries to ratify the Treaty. The EEC is now the EU.

↪ brexitchronicles.co.uk/mtc

With the acceptance of the Maastricht Treaty on 1 November 1993 the EU can now push ahead with its plans to implement a single currency (but not in the UK or Denmark).

> **'A referendum is a contradiction in a parliamentary democracy. We are elected to do the job.'**
> **Douglas Hurd MP**

BRIEF TIMELINE

11 December 1991 - John Major signs a draft of the MT

7 February 1992 - Douglas Hurd signs MT on behalf of UK

April 1992 - Conservatives win elections for a fourth term

21 May 1992 - Second reading MT Government wins 336 – 92

2 June 1992 - Denmark reject MT in a referendum

1 July 1992 - Britain has presidency of the EEC for 6 months

16 September 1992 - Britain forced to pull out of ERM

18 May 1993 - Denmark approves MT in a second referendum

20 May 1993 - Government wins third reading of MT 292-112

20 July 1993 - House of Lords approves MT 141 - 29

23 July 1993 - Government wins confidence vote on MT

2 August 1993 - Parliament ratifies MT with all other states

1 November 1993 - The Maastricht Treaty takes effect

The Concept of the Whip

The whip system has been around since 1884. Selected MPs or Members of the House of Lords can be a whip, their supervisor is the Chief Whip. Their task is to ensure that party members vote in alignment with party policies.

Whips have to inform MPs about upcoming debates and instruct them on how the party expects them to vote. They do this by sending out a letter (called The Whip) each week to all MPs. The Whip lists future debates and rates them by importance, shown by a number of underlines.

This method of bloc voting is there to promote discipline among MPs. You might consider this to be undemocratic but it's an attempt to get MPs to vote for the policies the Government was voted in on and not on the personal beliefs of each MP.

This system of underlining has three levels:

One-line whip - or one underline. This is only an advisory guideline with no consequences for those MPs who don't attend or vote. Should they decide to vote they are expected to vote as instructed.

Two-line whip - or two underlines, are more serious and an MP's attendance is 'necessary'. They are expected to vote as instructed and not doing so is frowned upon.

Three-line whip - or three underlines. This is a mandatory instruction to vote. This means the debate is very important to the party and is mostly reserved for votes on second readings of major bills or for votes of confidence.

The consequences for MPs who defy a three-line whip can be severe. This is where the term 'having the whip withdrawn' comes in, essentially it sacks an MP from the party, making them an independent until the whip is restored and they are let back into the party. Having the whip withdrawn can also mean losing your place in the Cabinet or being deselected, which means being sacked from the party altogether. Cabinet members are expected to resign first if they wish to vote against a three-line whip.

There have been occasions when whole groups of MPs have defied a three-line whip, resulting in them all having the whip withdrawn - as when John Major is faced with a vote of confidence or, later on, with Boris Johnson when 21 MPs abstain.

When the party in power has only a small majority in the House then the whips' job becomes much more important and disciplinary actions can be more severe.

May 1994 - Channel Tunnel officially open

Agreed in principle in 1876, Her Majesty the Queen and President Mitterrand open the Channel Tunnel on 6 May 1994.

 brexitchronicles.co.uk/ec/ET

June 1994 - Elections to European Parliament

The Conservative Government is becoming more and more unpopular as crisis after crisis hits. Major, with a 'wait and see' attitude, is undecided on whether to join the euro. Some of his critics believe that ruling out the single currency altogether may cost them the next election.

Elections to the European Parliament (EP) on 9 June 1994 are a disaster for the Conservatives, who get the lowest share of votes in a national election since 1832.

Labour is a clear winner with 62 seats, followed by the Conservatives with 18 seats. The Liberal Democrats manage two seats and UKIP, with only 1% of the votes, has no MEPs at all.

The split over Europe in the Conservative party is very present. They lost a number of senior ministers over the previous decade as a direct result of European policy: Michael Heseltine (1986); Nigel Lawson (1989); Nicholas Ridley (1990); and Geoffrey Howe (1990). Over the coming years there'll be many defections to other parties over disagreements on European issues. But what comes next is unexpected.

On the same day as the European elections Nigel Farage aged 30, stands in the Eastleigh by-election in Hampshire getting just 952 (1.7%) of the votes. A traditional Conservative safe seat, it is taken by the Lib-Dems receiving 44.3% against the Conservative coming third with 24.7% of the votes.

Nov. 1994 - Passing the European finance bill (EFB)

The Tory Rebels, as they are now called, are holding meetings during the October Party Conference, and plot their opposition to the EFB on 28 November 1994.

The EFB proposes increasing contribution payments by £75 million/year in 1995, rising to £250 million/year by 2000. This had been negotiated back in December 1992, when the UK held the EEC Presidency.

John Major makes it clear that this vote is an issue of confidence and carries a three-line whip. He also threatens that the consequence of not voting is losing the whip.

On the second reading of the bill in Parliament, Major wins the vote with a clear majority of 27. The bill passes.

Eight Tory Rebels abstain on a Labour amendment, which results in them having the whip withdrawn. A ninth rebel allegedly resigns the party whip of his own accord.

Major's reaction is unprecedented, after all, they hadn't actually voted against the Government, they'd abstained, and the bill had passed with a comfortable majority. The action of withdrawing the whip en masse results in Major now presiding over a minority Government.

A month later right-wing Conservatives begin a campaign to reinstate the Tory Rebels. The Conservative whip is eventually restored to all nine MPs on 24 April 1995.

November 1994 - Enter the Referendum Party

As John Major deals with party discord, businessman and billionaire Sir James Goldsmith launches the Referendum Party on 28 November 1994. This party only has one policy: to force an in-out referendum. It contests over 500 seats in the May 1997 general election and spends more on advertising than the Conservatives and Labour put together. They receive just under 3% of the votes and win no seats. What makes Goldsmith interesting? He is part of an elite that is questioning the motives of the EU.

↳ brexitchronicles.co.uk/ce/JG

↳ brexitchronicles.co.uk/ec/jgs

Unfortunately, Goldsmith dies just two months after the May 1997 elections, which results in the break-up of the party. Some supporters go on to create a Eurosceptic pressure group called the Democracy Movement, others join the newly formed UK Independence Party (UKIP).

What Goldsmith did achieve was mainstream newspapers giving more coverage to the Eurosceptic stance and influencing public opinion with regard to the Maastricht Treaty and adopting the euro.

November 1994 - Court of Auditors report

The European Court of Auditors' report on the financial state of the EU alleges that 10% of the budget is lost due to fraud and waste. This draws attention to the most important weaknesses in relation to spending in East Central Europe, and to the failure of the European Parliament to enforce competitive tenders for its Brussels building programme.

MP Bill Cash (Tory Rebel) seizes on the report to argue that 'British tax payers were contributing to a bottomless fraudulent pit'. The Commission is quick to point out that the 482-page report is neither comprehensive nor balanced.

Nov. 1994 - Norway again rejects joining EU by 52.2%

June 1995 - John Major battles for party leadership

Critics of Major doubt that he's capable of uniting the party over the issue of Europe. Major throws down the gauntlet during a press conference with the infamous words, 'Put up or shut up'. Conservative Eurosceptic MP John Redwood resigns as Secretary of State for Wales and challenges John Major for the position of Party Leader. Some big guns back him - Lord (Norman) Tebbit and former Chancellor, Norman Lamont. Redwood's campaign is based on his belief that Major is an electoral liability and the best chance for MPs to retain their seats lies in the appointment of a new leader. John Major announces his resignation as Party Leader on 22 June 1995 to face off against a single challenger.

As there are only two candidates the winner requires 50% of the votes plus a mandatory 15% more than their opponent - about 190 votes.

In the first ballot Major receives 218 votes (66%) against Redwood's 89. Major has a Cabinet reshuffle, which doesn't include Mr Redwood.

March 1996 - EC bans British beef

After Health Secretary Stephen Dorrell's speech in Parliament claiming there is a link between Creutzfeldt-Jakob disease and bovine spongiform encephalopathy (BSE or, more popularly, mad cow disease), the European Commission (EC) bans the export of British beef to Europe. British beef is then banned worldwide and by the end of 1997 over a million cattle have been destroyed.

In retaliation for the EU ban on beef exports, John Major announces on 21 May that the UK will veto all EU decisions that require unanimous support. Nigel Farage's first European Parliament speech is about beef.

⤷ brexitchronicles.co.uk/ec/BE

Later in 1996, Conservative Paymaster General David Heathcoat-Amory resigns, citing Major's refusal to rule out Britain's future membership of the single currency, and Lord McAlpine, a former Conservative party treasurer, defects to the Referendum Party.

John Major prorogues Parliament 19 days early

Major announces an election for 1 May 1997 as he has a minority Government (of -1) following the death of MP Iain Mills in January.

John Major controversially prorogues parliament on 21 March (19 days earlier than it would normally be dissolved for an election) to avoid an embarrassing parliamentary debate on the cash-for-questions affair.

In a successful sting operation by The Sunday Times in July 1994 journalists approach Conservative MPs, asking them to submit questions to Parliament in exchange for cash payments. The Guardian later reports on two other Tory MPs who took bribes to table questions on behalf of Harrods tycoon Mohamed Al-Fayed. After these incidents Major sets up the Nolan Committee on Standards in Public Life.

The cash-for-questions scandal had been front page news three years earlier and the timing of Major's prorogation held up publication of a damning report and delayed a debate just prior to a general election - when the last thing you want is stories about Conservative MPs taking bribes. Whether or not that was his intention is debatable.

Years later, Sir John Major joins a court case to reverse Boris Johnson's prorogation of Parliament over 9-12 September 2019, just four days before party conference season begins.

 brexitchronicles.co.uk/ce/JP

May 1997 - Labour wins 179-seat majority

After a rebrand as 'New Labour' the charismatic new party leader, Tony Blair aged just 43, ends 18 years of Labour Opposition. Labour wins 418 seats; the Liberal Democrats (led by Paddy Ashdown) double their position with 46 seats; the Conservatives are left with just 165 - a massive shift.

The Labour manifesto contains five main policies and talks a lot about Conservative broken promises. They promise a referendum on an EU single currency:

'We will give Britain the leadership in Europe which Britain and Europe need.'

'We will stand up for Britain's interests in Europe after the shambles of the last six years, but, more than that, we will lead a campaign for reform in Europe. Europe isn't working in the way this country and Europe need.'

A party political broadcast for the Labour Party explains their five-point manifesto.

↪ brexitchronicles.co.uk/LP

A two-part programme talks about the day after the election.

↪ brexitchronicles.co.uk/ec/EL

↪ brexitchronicles.co.uk/LW

CHAPTER FIVE

THE BLUNDER YEARS

May 1997 - Manifesto promises new life for Britain

Some key parts of the 1996 Labour manifesto that led to a landslide victory:

'We oppose a European federal superstate.'

'Lead reform of the EU.'

'We have set out a detailed agenda for reform, leading from the front during the UK presidency in the first half of 1998.'

'**Rapid completion of the single market**: We will open up markets to competition; pursue tough action against unfair state aid; and ensure proper enforcement of single market rules.'

'**High priority for enlargement** of the European Union to include the countries of central and eastern Europe and Cyprus.'

'**Urgent reform of the Common Agricultural Policy**. It is costly, vulnerable to fraud and not geared to environmental protection. Enlargement and the World Trade talks in 1999 will make reform even more essential. We will seek a thorough overhaul of the Common Fisheries Policy to conserve our fish stocks in the long-term interests of the UK fishing industry.'

'**Greater openness and democracy in EU institutions** with open voting in the Council of Ministers and more effective scrutiny of the Commission by the European Parliament.'

'**Retention of the national veto over key matters** of national interest, such as taxation, defence and security, immigration, decisions over the budget and treaty changes.'

'**Britain to sign the Social Chapter.** An empty chair at the negotiating table is disastrous for Britain. The Social Chapter is a framework under which legislative measures can be agreed. Only two measures have been agreed. The Social Chapter cannot be used to force the harmonisation of social security [which is higher in Germany for example] or tax legislation and it does not cost jobs. We will use our participation to promote employability and flexibility, not high social costs.'

Referendum on adopting a single currency

The manifesto states:

'Any decision about Britain joining the single currency must be determined by a hard-headed assessment of Britain's economic interests. Only Labour can be trusted to do this. But there are formidable obstacles in the way of Britain being in the first wave of membership if economic and monetary union (EMU) takes place on 1 January 1999 (actually launched in 1992). What is essential for the success of EMU is genuine convergence among the economies that take part, without any fudging of the rules. However, to exclude British membership of EMU forever would be to destroy any influence we have over a process which will affect us whether we are in or out. We must therefore play a full part in the debate to influence it in Britain's interests.'

'In any event, there are three pre-conditions which would have to be satisfied before Britain could join during the next Parliament: first, the Cabinet would have to agree; then Parliament; and finally, the people would have to say "Yes" in a referendum.'

> **No such referendum ever took place**

Tony Blair's first Prime Minister's Questions (PMQs)
on 21 May 1997

⤷   brexitchronicles.co.uk/ce/pmq

After the sudden death of Labour leader John Smith in May 1994, Tony Blair is elected Leader of the Opposition, defeating John Prescott and Margaret Beckett. Straight away he re-brands the party, giving it the name 'New Labour'. Smith's cautious approach of keeping a low profile and banking on the unpopularity of the Conservatives to give Labour an election win is not Blair's style.

Blair was born into working-class surroundings in Edinburgh. The family moved to Adelaide, Australia, before his second birthday then returned to the UK some four years later.

At nineteen he studies law at Oxford and graduates in 1975 with a second-class Honours BA in jurisprudence. A short time later he joins the Labour party and puts himself forward as a councillor in 1982 but isn't selected. He then runs in a by-election in the safe Conservative seat of Beaconsfield, and loses.

The Conservatives see an advantage in changing constituency boundaries, which creates the new constituency of Sedgefield, County Durham. A number of Labour MPs make a grab for the seat, but Blair approaches the local Labour branch and convinces the branch secretary to nominate him. Blair, aged 30, wins the seat in the 1983 election and receives his first front-bench appointment a year later as assistant Treasury spokesman. He continues on up through the ranks and becomes Shadow Home Secretary under John Smith before becoming Leader.

One of Blair's key moves is the decision not to let go of Thatcher's economic policies but to expand on them. Nationalization of everything that moves, a Labour cornerstone, is now off the agenda. Thatcherism had changed the very fabric of society, and things like privatization are no longer frowned upon - especially among those who had benefited from the purchase of a council house.

On the upside, Blair introduces the national minimum wage and national programmes to end poverty.

When Blair takes power in May 1997 net migration to the UK is about 48,000, a year later it jumps to around 140,000 and never goes below 100,000 per year thereafter. People in EU countries discover the benefits of living in the UK.

As a pro-European Tony Blair very quickly delivers on his manifesto promise and signs Britain up to the Social Chapter on 18 June 1997.

June 1997 - John Major steps down

William Hague takes over as Conservative Party Leader at the age of 36. He beats two experienced Cabinet members, Kenneth Clarke (57) and Michael Howard (56). He must now resurrect a party that had suffered its worst ever defeat.

Just two years later he succeeds in beating Labour at the European parliamentary elections with 36 MEPs to Labour's 29.

July 1997 - Agenda 2000 tabled by EC

The Agenda 2000 programme, tabled by the EC, sets out a blueprint to establish a new financial framework in preparation for EU enlargement. The level of structural and cohesion funding is to be paired with proposed cuts of 20% in the cereal support price in the year 2000, a reduction of 30% in the beef intervention price between 2000 and 2002, and a 10% decline in the support price for milk. These cutbacks will take place against the backdrop of a new world trade agreement which will seek to eliminate export refunds. This is the first attempt to cut subsidies to farmers.

October 1997 - Treaty of Amsterdam signed

This is the first attempt to update the Maastricht Treaty and to prepare for the future accession of ten new member states. It takes two years of negotiations before all 12 States sign - the UK now adopts the Social Chapter.

The treaty also introduces the idea of a two-speed Europe, allowing countries that want to forge ahead with a closer union to do so.

The Schengen agreement later becomes law and gets rid of internal border checks for all member states - except for Britain and Ireland who opted out. Most importantly, it increases the Union's powers and removes some executive powers from the European Council and gives them to the Commission.

In the lead-up to the Treaty of Amsterdam four countries hold a referendum in preparation for joining the EU:

Austria, June 1994, votes to join by 66.6% (82% turnout)
Finland, October 1994, votes to join by 56.9%
Åland Islands (Finland), November 1994, votes to join by 73.6%
Sweden, November 1994, votes to join by 52.3%.

Two member states hold referendums on the ratification of the Treaty of Amsterdam:

Ireland, May 1998, votes in favour by 61.7%
Denmark, May 1998, votes in favour by 55.1% (76.2% turnout).

There are referendums and EUphoria (sorry) among countries keen to join and member states keen to have them join.

On 30 October 1997 the UK gives the EU Council notice that it will not be adopting the single currency on 1 January 1999. It also reserves the right to adopt it at a later date.

The predecessor to the euro, known as the EMU, was a virtual currency only used for commercial and financial transactions. It had been adopted by 11 of the 15 member states. By 1 January 2002, 12 member states have adopted the euro as legal tender and begin to phase out their own national currency.

Whereas Britain and Denmark opt out, Sweden refuses to meet the criteria, disallowing its implementation.

Corruption scandal forces entire EC to resign

The European Commission helps shape the EU's overall strategy, proposes new laws and policies, monitors their implementation, and manages the budget and day-to-day business of the EU. It employs around 32,000 civil servants to carry out these duties.

On 15 July 1994, the European Council appoints Jacques Santer, ex-Prime Minister of Luxembourg, as President of the European Commission (known as the Santer Commission, 23 January 1995-15 March 1999). The selection of 20 committee members falls to the Commission President, under Maastricht Treaty rules which require only EU Parliamentary endorsement.

The Santer Commission's document entitled Agenda 2000, proposes a radical reform of the common agricultural policy (CAP), and to make structural funds more efficient as enlargement of the Union approaches.

The Commission is scrutinized by the European Parliament, who refuse to sign off their accounts for the 1996 financial year. Articles appear in German and Scandinavian newspapers about undue payments to certain MEPs.

In 1999 the entire European Union Executive Commission is forced to resign by the EU Parliament after a scathing report on corruption. The internal auditor of the Commission's financial control unit, Mr. Paul van Buitenen, discovers a series of irregularities with regard to payments of allowances.

He accuses the French EU Commissioner Édith Cresson of serious and repeated fraud, of falsifying contracts, of forging signatures and of embezzling EU funds. She hires René Berthelot, a dental surgeon and close friend, to be a highly paid EU adviser on HIV/Aids. Berthelot was later judged to be unqualified, over two years he had produced 24 pages of notes of little or no value. In 2006, the European Court of Justice finds that Mrs. Cresson had acted in breach of her obligations as European Commissioner. Manuel Marin, the Spanish Commissioner, was also found guilty of fraud in relation to humanitarian aid. Jacques Santer does not remove either Commissioner.

Other Commission members are now being investigated. At a meeting of the Commission they decide to all resign together.

↳ brexitchronicles.co.uk/ce/SA

Next comes the Prodi Commission, led by former Italian PM Romano Prodi (1999-2004). Four members of the Santer Commission, including ex-Labour Leader Neil Kinnock, are reappointed to the committee. The Amsterdam Treaty had increased the Commission's powers to such an extent that the press dubbed Prodi as being akin to the first EU Prime Minister.

The Barroso Commission follows (2004-2014). Here's an audit from Nigel Farage about the choice of committee members.

↳ brexitchronicles.co.uk/ec/TD

Who is opting out of what?

To allow the EU agenda to move forward when countries cannot or will not adopt parts of a treaty, those countries are given the right to opt-out. Once a member state is granted an opt-out it's permanent until that country decides to opt-in. This avoids an overall stalemate and creates a two-speed Europe. This is cherry picking you might say.

Examples of opt-outs include:

➢ Schengen Agreement: Ireland and the UK

➢ Economic and monetary union: Denmark and the UK

➢ Defence: Denmark

➢ EU Charter of Fundamental Rights: Poland and the UK

➢ Area of freedom, security and justice: Denmark, Ireland and the UK

Closer unification of member states is scheduled for the year 2020. Will all EU members then have to adopt the euro?

The UK and Denmark opt-outs exclude membership of the euro currency. A member state can decide to relinquish any of its opt-outs, but the EU can't currently force a country to surrender them.

As you see, the UK has opted-out of quite a few things.

April 1998 - Signing the Good Friday Agreement (GFA)

There has been conflict in Ireland ever since Oliver Cromwell, Lord Protector of England, marched into Ireland in August 1649 to wage war against the Roman Catholics. (Cromwell, by the way, established the precedent that an English monarch requires consent from Parliament to rule, which still stands.)

The 1921 split that created the Irish Free State and a Northern Ireland with direct rule from Westminster caused more than a century of unrest between Britain and Ireland.

I remember scenes of violence on the television during the 1960s and 1970s as armed groups on both sides carried out deadly bombings in Britain and Northern Ireland. Margaret Thatcher's campaign manager and spokesman on Northern Ireland, Mr Airey Neave, was assassinated by an Irish National Liberation Army car bomb outside Westminster. Imprisoned members of the Irish Republican Army (IRA) went on hunger strike in a bid to get prisoner-of-war status and ten died. With Bloody Sundays and Bloody Fridays, it seemed like there would never be an end to the troubles.

The breakthrough comes on 31 August 1994, when the IRA declares a ceasefire and the bombings and shootings stop. This allows negotiations to open up that culminate in the IRA signing the Good Friday Agreement (The Belfast Agreement) at 5:30 pm on Friday 10 April 1998, ratified by referendums that put an end to the Northern Ireland conflict.

It is no doubt one of the most important documents created for achieving peace within the United Kingdom and the Republic of Ireland (ROI). Here is an extract from Article 1:

Two Governments:

(i) recognise the legitimacy of whatever choice is freely exercised by a majority of the people of Northern Ireland with regard to its status, whether they prefer to continue to support the Union with Great Britain or a sovereign united Ireland;

(ii) recognise that it is for the people of the island of Ireland alone, by agreement between the two parts respectively and without external impediment, to exercise their right of self-determination on the basis of consent, freely and concurrently given, North and South, to bring about a united Ireland, if that is their wish, accepting that this right must be achieved and exercised with and subject to the agreement and consent of a majority of the people of Northern Ireland;

(iii) acknowledge that while a substantial section of the people in Northern Ireland share the legitimate wish of a majority of the people of the island of Ireland for a united Ireland, the present wish of a majority of the people of Northern Ireland, freely exercised and legitimate, is to maintain the Union and accordingly, that Northern Ireland's status as part of the United Kingdom reflects and relies upon that wish; and that it would be wrong to make any change in the status of Northern Ireland save with the consent of a majority of its people;

The agreement creates the Northern Ireland Assembly to allow some self-rule. It is the start of devolution within the United Kingdom - later, Scotland and Wales get their own Parliaments. Although ongoing disagreements between the main parties cause the Northern Ireland Assembly to collapse in January 2017 the agreement still stands.

An open border between Northern Ireland and the ROI is an important part of the peace process to appease the IRA's goal of a united Ireland. Article 1 recognises the legitimacy of the desire for a united Ireland, while declaring that it can only be achieved through a referendum. Such a referendum would most likely fail as the majority of people in Northern Ireland are Protestants in favour of continued union with Great Britain.

When Northern Ireland and the ROI joined the European Single Market in 1992 checks on goods at the border are phased out and give the feeling of a single country. The 1998 GFA then de-escalates the conflict to a point where a militarized border is no longer necessary. This is the invisible, frictionless border that all now want to defend, although there is no specific mention of open borders in the GFA.

Tensions have not gone away, and people still live segregated lives, kids attend non-secular schools and play different sports. Fortunately, the riots, bomb blasts and sniper fire that have claimed the lives of some 3,600 people are a thing of the past. Anything that jeopardizes this fragile truce could mean the return of violence and killings that many would rather forget.

September 2000 - Danish euro referendum

Denmark, 28 September 2000, 53.2% against, turnout 87.6%

They'd opted out of the euro when signing the Maastricht Treaty, but could later chose to put it to the people. The turnout of over 87% is very high and the people say no.

February 2001 - Treaty of Nice signed

To facilitate EU enlargement by a further ten states, which will add 70 million people to its ranks, the Treaty of Nice agrees to limited institutional adaptations - especially on voting rules in Council and proposals to reduce the number of Commissioners.

The plan is for ten countries to join the EU in 2004: Poland, Hungary, Lithuania, Latvia, Estonia, Slovenia, Slovakia, Czech Republic, Malta and Cyprus. Membership of the EU would then be 25 countries with 456 million people.

The system in which all 12 member states have to agree unanimously leads to very watered-down policies. With 25+ states this would be even worse, so the Treaty of Nice calls for a qualified majority when voting (QMV).

This treaty is very much about a balance of power within the EU. Germany pushes to have more say, arguing that its 82 million inhabitants should give it more voting power than the UK, with only 60 million. The Netherlands with 15 million inhabitants has the same issue with regard to Belgium, with only 10 million. Brussels rejects the idea of having less power than its northern neighbour. This results in: Germany, France, the United Kingdom, and Italy getting 29 votes each; Spain and Poland getting 27 votes; and other countries getting progressively fewer votes depending on population size.

No single member can veto a proposal. A veto requires at least 62% of the Union's population. This means that a combination of the four 'big' states is enough to veto anything.

It is the same with the allocation of 732 seats for MEPs. Germany can elect 99 MEPs, France, the United Kingdom, and Italy get 72 each. Spain and Poland get 50 seats, the rest get progressively fewer seats according to population.

The treaty calls for enhanced competencies of the President of the EC, who now has to be elected by a qualified majority and be ratified by the European Parliament.

An Irish referendum in June 2001 rejects the Nice Treaty by 54%, but a second referendum in October 2002 passes it. Denmark and France also ratify it via referendums.

This treaty gives the EU permission to bring in new members, including Eastern Bloc countries, who will require financial aid for many years. A treaty driven mostly by Germany's Chancellor Helmut Kohl, who sees the benefits of having cheap production facilities and cheaper labour on his doorstep.

 ↳ brexitchronicles.co.uk/CL

Labour Prime Minister Tony Blair doesn't see the need for a referendum. On the bill's third reading it is passed by 392 to 158 votes. More than 100 MPs don't bother to vote at all. Given Labour's huge majority the result is easy to foresee. Secretary of State Jack Straw opposes a referendum, citing:

'The idea to hold a referendum on the Nice Treaty is absurd and contradictory to British tradition.'
Secretary of State Jack Straw

So, according to Jack Straw MP (Lab) there's a British 'tradition' of not giving the people a say on such matters.

Ratification by all other states happens without major difficulties and all are carried out via parliamentary procedure.

Treaty of Nice comes into force on 1 February 2003

June 2001 - Labour wins election with 165 majority

Voter turnout is 12% down on the previous election. With just five fewer seats, Labour are in a great position to push policy through the House. Labour end their first term promise to match the Conservatives on public spending. Gordon Brown, Chancellor of the Exchequer, now goes on a spending spree and increases budgets for the NHS, schools, and other public services.

William Hague has not managed to lift the Conservative Party out of the doldrums, they only win 165 seats. The party is deeply divided on the EU and perceived by the public as shifting too far to the right. After three months Hague resigns, and Tory rebel Iain Duncan Smith becomes party leader.

No fewer than two future Conservative Prime Ministers become new MPs: David Cameron and Boris Johnson.

Watch Tony Blair seeking re-election and sharing his views on the UK and Europe.

 brexitchronicles.co.uk/ids

January 2002 - Euro becomes cross-Europe currency

The UK is one of the few countries to remain outside the euro.

Referendums to join EU held in all these countries

Malta, March 2003 - 53.6% in favour, turnout 90.9%

Slovenia, March 2003 - 89.6% in favour, turnout 60.2%

Hungary, April 2003 - 83.8% in favour, turnout 45.6%

Lithuania, May 2003 - 91.9% in favour, turnout 63.4%

Slovakia, May 2003 - 93.7% in favour, turnout 52.1%

Poland, June 2003 - 77.5% in favour, turnout 58.9%

Czech Republic, June 2003 - 77.3% in favour, turnout 55.2%

Estonia, September 2003 - 66.8% in favour, turnout 64.1%

Latvia, September 2003 - 67.5% in favour, turnout 71.5%

From Iraq war to the Chilcot report

Blair agrees to launch attacks on Iraq with the USA and creates a legacy of regret that lessens his popularity. This is the last election to give any party a majority of more than 100 seats. Here is the story from bombing Iraq to the Chilcot report.

↪ brexitchronicles.co.uk/ce/lie

April 2003 - Ten states sign Treaty of Accession

The Treaty of Accession defines conditions for the ten new member states when they join the EU. The Maastricht Treaty says that all new members are obliged to adopt the euro. Only seven (Estonia, Cyprus, Latvia, Lithuania, Malta, Slovenia, Slovakia) qualify to join the eurozone (the group name for members that adopt the euro), three don't.

The Czech Republic, Hungary and Poland don't meet the Maastricht criteria for joining the eurozone or the EU, but are nevertheless allowed in - by 2019 there is still no target date for them to adopt the euro.

Annual opinion polls in the Czech Republic over the last ten years show that a referendum is likely to end in the euro being rejected by at least 60% of the population.

Sept. 2003 - Swedish referendum says no to euro

Sweden, September 2003, 55.9% against, turnout 82.6%

June 2004 - EC Constitution proposal

The European Commission under Romano Prodi starts the Penelope Project in 2001. This is a plan to create a single constitution to replace all existing treaties and to define more clearly who does what in the EU. Sold by the EC as an innocent 'tidying-up exercise' to make the EU more workable, it is undoubtedly a massive grab for power.

Critics of the Penelope Project see it as an attempt to give more powers to the Commission relative to Parliament and Council. The final draft includes the position of President of the European Union.

The EU would become a sovereign entity with a governing body in its own right; and the European Court of Justice would become the EU Supreme Court. The big winners would be MEPs, who would gain power to fast track constitutional change as referendum failures in member states during ratification would not veto a policy, given the introduction of qualified majority voting (QMV).

QMV means 'at least 55% of the members of the Council, comprising at least fifteen of them and representing member states comprising at least 65% of the population of the Union'.

In my opinion, the ramifications of the Penelope Project are more far-reaching than I have described as I believe it is an attempt to create a federal state. Step by step, power would shift from member states as Parliament and Council become QMV-driven and more powerful. It was the concept of QMV that prompted Margaret Thatcher's 'no, no, no' speech.

This treaty establishing an 'EU Constitution' is adopted by the European Council on 18 June 2004 and is signed in Rome on 29 October 2004 by all representatives of the 25 member states of the EU. It then has to be ratified by all 25 members, either through a referendum or by parliamentary procedure.

It is overwhelmingly passed by 16 member states - the number of parliamentarians against it are in the single digits.

It is written into the treaty with Bulgaria and Romania when they join in 2005. They automatically agree.

May 2005, in France's referendum, 54.68% vote against the treaty. Tony Blair comments on the French vote.

↳   brexitchronicles.co.uk/ce/EA

Two days later the Netherlands referendum shows a worse result, with 61.54% of voters against ratifying the EU Constitutional Treaty. On the basis of these results, seven countries, including the UK, cancel their planned referendums.

How Blair deals with the EU Constitution Treaty

20 April 2004 - Tony Blair announces his intention to hold a referendum, without giving a date. Eight other member states announce that they will hold referendums on the EU Constitution Treaty. In view of the UK Government's massive majority, and to not go against a British 'tradition', why would they want a referendum?

The new Labour Foreign Secretary, Jack Straw, is the driving force for a referendum within the Cabinet (yes, the same Jack Straw). He says the vote would have 'wider implications' for Britain's relationship with Europe but would not be a choice between being 'in or out'. He insists that Tony Blair would not have to resign if he lost.

Mr Blair says in Parliament: 'It is time to resolve once and for all whether this country, Britain, wants to be at the centre and heart of European decision-making or not. Time to decide whether our destiny lies as a leading partner and ally in Europe or on its margins. Let the issue be put and let the battle be joined.'

He says the choice would become very clear as the debate continued - between Britain playing its full part in the EU or going down a road favoured by the Conservatives, which would 'change fundamentally' its relationship with Europe.

Take the above speech in the context of what we now know, that Blair had ambitions to become EU President.

I can only imagine that the Labour Cabinet and eight other member states realized that this was a treaty of such magnitude, that it would change their constitution to such a degree that they had to protect themselves from any negative consequences, and that only a referendum could do that.

Eight other EU states, six of which had never had an EU referendum, were also planning to give the people a voice for the first time.

April 2004 - Tony Blair on migration

Immigration is becoming a big issue with the general public after scandals about migrant abuse of the system touch on the British sense of genuine unfairness. This, coupled with a looming election, inspire Tony Blair to make a speech outlining the Government's immigration strategy.

During the ten years of Tony Blair's tenure, over two million more migrants than the Government had expected come to Britain. As there is no clear policy on integration new arrivals tend to live in communities of their own kind. Blair does not see the mass influx of people as an issue. He dismisses as 'racist' the Tory warnings about Third World economic migrants entering Britain as tourists and then claiming asylum. The Home Office reckons that in 1995 asylum-seekers had claimed more than £200 million in benefits - yet only 5% were genuine refugees.

However, Blair does recognize a problem with bogus asylum seekers, and it becomes an election issue after 1999. He converts over 350,000 asylum-seekers into economic migrants, gives them work permits, and rights to social benefits.

This gives an impression that the UK is a soft touch, which results in thousands of illegal immigrants heading over.

Here is the speech in full.

↳ brexitchronicles.co.uk/IM

May 2005 - Labour wins historic third term

Not by as large a majority as four years earlier, but winning 355 seats. The Conservatives have 198 and the Liberal Democrats 62, which still leaves Labour with a comfortable majority.

Last PMQs before the 2005 election.

↳ brexitchronicles.co.uk/ec/PB

A 2005 party political broadcast on behalf of UKIP.

↳ brexitchronicles.co.uk/ce/UP

Every party's 2005 election manifesto offers a referendum on the EU constitutional treaty.

Labour says: 'We will put it (the constitutional treaty) to the British people in a referendum and campaign whole-heartedly for a "Yes" vote to keep Britain a leading nation in Europe.'

The Labour manifesto says the constitutional treaty: sets out what the EU can and cannot do; strengthens the voice of national parliaments and governments in EU affairs; and ensures that Britain keeps control of key national interests like foreign policy, taxation, social security, and defence.

The Conservative view is: 'We oppose the EU Constitution and would give the British people the chance to reject its provisions in a referendum within six months of the general election.'

The Liberal Democrats are 'clear in our support for the constitution, which we believe is in Britain's interest - but ratification must be subject to a referendum of the British people'.

> **For all three major parties to be this much in favour of a referendum it must be really important**

EU Constitution set aside

It all falls apart as European leaders announce plans to set the EU Constitution aside for a 'period of reflection' as the Dutch and French referendums hinder ratification, which requires all member states to sign up to the treaty.

This is not the end of the EU Constitution - by no means!

Romano Prodi steps down as EC President in October 2004 to be replaced by José Manuel Barroso in November 2004. The Barroso Commission revives the EU Constitution and begins to mull over ways to make it acceptable. A State of the Union Address by Barroso in 2012 openly says: 'We will need to move towards a federation of nation states.'

July-December 2005 - UK EU Presidency

With Tony Blair as President of the Council of the EU for the next six months, Britain could push policy in her favour.

In the final month of his presidency, Tony Blair agrees to give up 20% (£7 billion per year) of Britain's rebate (as negotiated by Margaret Thatcher). These are extra funds the EU needs to help prop up failing economies, but they are listed as modernization funds for the eight eastern European newcomers - to the tune of €862 billion of taxpayers' money for 2007-2013. However, for the first time the deal does raise France's contribution to be equal to Britain's.

Nigel Farage, at the European Parliament on 20 December 2005, can hardly contain himself as he aims a speech at the blunders of Tony Blair.

   brexitchronicles.co.uk/BP

Dec. 2005 - Cameron becomes Conservative Leader

After their defeat in the May 2005 elections, Michael Howard steps down and David Cameron becomes Leader of the Conservative Party on 6 December 2005.

See Cameron on his first day in Parliament as Opposition Leader questioning Tony Blair.

   brexitchronicles.co.uk/CB

EU Constitution revived by Amato Group

Millions of euros had been spent on creating the EU Constitution that was defeated by the Dutch and French referendums, but the Commission is not going to be deterred.

Now driven by the Barroso Commission, there's an unofficial meeting on 30 September 2006 in Rome. As part of the 'reflection period' a group of 16 'wise men' - consisting of MEPs, former prime ministers, and members of the EC - sit down to consider the next course of action to revive the EU Constitution.

These wise men include: Costas Simitis, former Prime Minister of Greece; Dominique Strauss-Kahn, Managing Director of the International Monetary Fund (IMF); Otto Schily, former German Interior Minister accused of receiving money to lobby for the prosecution in Austria of Rakhat Aliyev in 2015; Chris Patten, British Lord, European Commissioner and the last Governor of Hong Kong; they are led by former Italian Prime Minister Giuliano Amato, hence the name of Amato Group.

They decide that the best way forward is to take the parts of the EU Constitution that nobody objects to and get it passed as a new treaty. Those parts that are not being agreed to would be tabled as lots of amendments to the Treaty of Rome and the Maastricht Treaty.

By the end of 2007 they are ready and change the name, EU Constitution, to something far less threatening. As the place of signing is Barroso's home town, it becomes the Lisbon Treaty.

Sept. 2006 - Pressure group 'Better Off Out' launched

A non-party campaign brings together prominent people from both sides of the House as the Better Off Out group. Their only aim is the UK's withdrawal from the EU. Supporters include Lord Tebbit, former DUP leader Ian Paisley, MP Peter Bone (Con), MP David Davies (Con), and Christopher Gill.

September 2006 - Nigel Farage elected UKIP Leader

On 12 September 2006 Nigel Farage is elected Leader of the UK Independence party, replacing Roger Knapman.

Nigel Farage left the Conservative Party in 1992 as a result of John Major signing the Maastricht Treaty. He becomes a founding member of UKIP in 1994 and MEP for South East England in the 1999 European Parliament elections.

Farage has running battles with EC President José Manuel Barroso from 2004. In 2005 Farage tables a vote of no confidence, accusing Barroso of misconduct.

First interview with Farage after becoming UKIP Party Leader.

  brexitchronicles.co.uk/ec/KP

May 2007 - Tony Blair announces step down

Blair never recovered his popularity after instigating the Iraq war, based on false information from Germany about weapons of mass destruction, and his party see him as an electoral liability. On the tenth anniversary of the general election that swept him to power he announces his departure and endorses Gordon Brown as his successor. Blair had made it clear in 2004 that he had no intention of standing for a fourth term as leader.

Tony Blair's last PMQs on 27 June 2007. The question from Sir Nicholas Winterton (Con) (at 24 minutes) calls for a referendum, citing the new Treaty (of Lisbon), which is, in substance, the old discredited Constitutional Treaty.

Blair finishes his PMQs with: 'Parliament is still the arena that sets the heart beating a little faster and if it is on occasions the place of low skulduggery, it is more often the place for the pursuit of noble causes.'

↳ brexitchronicles.co.uk/ce/YP

Brown's only contender for PM is MP John McDonnel, but he fails to get enough nominations for a place on the ballot and concedes defeat. On 24 June 2007 Gordon Brown is declared the new Labour Leader to replace the increasingly unpopular Tony Blair.

As with John Major, Brown is not leader through the democratic process of the British electorate but through selection by a Labour party vote.

December 2007 - Lisbon Treaty signed

The Lisbon Treaty is signed by the 27 EU members, which starts the process of ratification, either by referendum or by parliamentary vote.

The Lisbon Treaty replaces the rejected EU Constitution that had compelled nine countries to hold a referendum, given its far-reaching consequences on the constitutions of all 27 member states. This Treaty keeps most of the old content but gives up any reference to the word 'constitution', saying it is only amending the Maastricht Treaty (1992) and the Treaty of Rome (1957) - 300 pages of amendments to 3,000 other pages of treaties. Nobody reads it, and nobody understands it!

I find statements from the EU such as, 'The Lisbon Treaty would give the European and national parliaments a bigger role in the decision-making process, and thus raise the EU's democratic profile', disconcerting. Does this mean ignoring referendums?

William Hague's slight on Tony Blair's ambition to be President of Europe and the ramifications of Gordon signing the Lisbon Treaty.

↳ brexitchronicles.co.uk/ec/LT

At the risk of being boring, it is still a requirement that ALL EU member states ratify a treaty before it can become law - either by holding a referendum or by parliamentary consent.

Having learnt the lesson that referendums just get in the way of true democracy, 26 member states simply don't hold one.

Only Ireland prepares to hold a referendum.

Amendment tabled to nullify the Irish referendum

In Strasbourg on 20 February 2008, the same day the EU parliament approves the Lisbon Treaty, they hold a debate on the Corbett-de Vigo Report, which proposes amendments that have to be voted on before the whole treaty is put to the vote.

To pre-empt a negative result from Ireland's referendum, amendment 32 asks that the European Parliament 'undertake to respect the outcome of the referendum in Ireland'. In other words, should the European Parliament respect the result of the forthcoming Irish referendum on the Lisbon Treaty?

**The amendment is rejected
by 499 votes to 129, only 33 abstain**

Even an Irish MEP - Proinsias de Rossa - votes not to respect his own country's referendum.

*This one action of the EU Parliament
nullifies a legitimate referendum,
demonstrating how the EU's
democratic profile could be raised.*

After the final vote on the Lisbon Treaty - 525 to 115 against, 29 abstentions - Hans-Gert Poettering, President of the European Parliament, ends the ceremony saying:

'A vast majority of you have voted in favour of the Lisbon Treaty. This is an expression of the free will of the people you represent (except the people were never asked). I'd like to congratulate you on this convincing result. This European Parliament represents the people of Europe, this treaty gives the European Union the ability to function properly and this treaty gives it more democracy. And we defend the common values of Europe and (referring to a few protesting MEPs) we shall never allow loud noise to override sensible arguments.'

So why wouldn't you ask yourself, what's the point of holding a referendum, the result of which has already been annulled? The European Parliament sent a clear message to the Irish people that, in the quest to ratify this treaty at any cost, they don't care what others have to say. A fine example of European democracy.

June 2008 - Irish referendum on Lisbon Treaty

Ireland's constitution requires that proposed amendments to the Constitution of Ireland must be decided upon and ratified by the people.

Ireland, June 2008, vote against by 53.4% (53.1% turnout)

↪ brexitchronicles.co.uk/IR

Respect the Irish Vote campaign started

A campaign is started in Brussels to 'Respect the Irish Vote'.

↳ brexitchronicles.co.uk/riv

One phrase comes up a few times from MEPs: 'We respect the vote of Ireland' (although they had just voted not to respect it).

Past behaviour of a parliament is a good indicator of its future behaviour. MEPs from Germany, Italy, France, and so on decide that the will of the Irish people should be annulled by a vote in the EU Parliament. Am I the only one who shudders at the consequences of this?

Sure there's uproar, but compared to how Sinn Féin would have reacted if the UK had done this, the response is mild.

What do you think would happen if the UK Parliament held a referendum, didn't like the result, then passed a bill in Parliament for 'more democratic accountability to respect the outcome of the referendum - aye or nay?' and then voted by 80% for no. Take a moment to consider how big the protest would be.

Is Nigel Farage the only EU critic? Interviews with Irish and Danish MEPs with an explanation of how QMV works.

↳ brexitchronicles.co.uk/ec/iid

October 2009 - Ireland's second referendum

The pretext is that Government had renegotiated the terms of the Treaty, so were presenting it to the Irish people to ask if Government could ratify it.

↳   brexitchronicles.co.uk/ce/isr

The referendum asks to amend the Constitution of Ireland to permit the state to ratify the Treaty of Lisbon.

This is not the same as asking if they agree with the Treaty.

Jeremy Corbyn - ‚A European empire of the 21st century'

↳   brexitchronicles.co.uk/ec/JD

Ireland, October 2009, vote in favour by 67.1% (59.0% turnout)

France and Denmark should have had referendums

France and Denmark, whose constitutions also require a referendum, and who both voted down the EU Constitution, are silenced.

February 2008, the French Parliament votes to amend the French Constitution to allow the Assemblée Nationale and the Senate to ratify the Lisbon Treaty. Mr Nicolas Sarkozy reassures French voters that this is a mini treaty, with the constitutional aspects of the old one (EU Constitution) stripped out.

In Denmark, Prime Minister Anders Fogh Rasmussen decides alone not to hold a referendum on the EU Lisbon Treaty, leaving it for MPs to ratify. The Treaty passes by 90 votes in favour and 25 against, 64 MPs out of the 179-seat parliament abstain. The Danish media portray PM Rasmussen as a possible candidate for President of the European Council if the Lisbon Treaty comes into force.

A class action lawsuit is filed in 2009 by 34 people who argue that because the Treaty affects Danish sovereignty on a number of issues, it should have been submitted to a referendum. On 15 June 2012 Denmark's High Court finds that the country's Government is not obliged to hold a referendum before signing the Lisbon Treaty.

> **There was only one referendum on the Lisbon Treaty**

How does the UK deal with ratification?

January 2008 - Cameron pledges poll on Lisbon Treaty

Right from the start, just a few weeks after Brown signs the Lisbon Treaty, Opposition Leader David Cameron makes a bold statement. If the Tories win the next election, he promises to hold a referendum on the Lisbon Treaty, if it has not already been ratified.

↪ brexitchronicles.co.uk/cpl

Gordon's Labour Government believes a referendum is not necessary as the UK has secured opt-outs and because most changes made by the Treaty are minor or procedural. Government's motion to ratify the Lisbon Treaty passes on 21 January 2008 by 362 to 224 votes. Royal assent is granted on 19 June 2008.

This Act doesn't actually ratify the treaty; it merely adds it to the treaties listed in the European Communities Act 1972. Ratification only takes place when Government deposits the ratification documents in Rome on 16 July 2008.

January 2008 - Black Monday

The Dow Jones falls by 12.8%, causing shock waves. This is followed by Black Tuesday, when the Dow falls a further 30.57 points.

March 2008 - Tories table referendum motion

Although the House had passed a motion to ratify the Lisbon Treaty back in January, the Tory Opposition table an amendment, calling for a vote on 5 March to allow a public referendum. They also support Ian Davidson (Labour backbencher), who additionally wants an in-out referendum on EU membership. Cameron appeals to Liberal Democrats to support a vote against their leader, Nick Clegg, in a final push to secure a referendum on the Lisbon Treaty.

'Every political party promised one at the last election and only the Conservative Party is sticking to its pledge and campaigning for that referendum.' Mr Cameron said, 'Voters would feel desperately let down if their MPs failed to honour previous election promises to give the people a say.'

Mr Clegg, a strong pro-European, causes a split in his party by saying that the public should be granted an in-out vote to clear the air on Europe once and for all. But he also argues that a vote on the Lisbon Treaty is not required as it doesn't make any significant constitutional changes.

> **British MPs reject the motion to hold a referendum on whether to ratify the Lisbon Treaty**

The House of Commons turns down the amendment by 311 votes to 248. Three Liberal Democrat frontbenchers - Alistair Carmichael, Tim Farron and David Heath - resign after defying the party's order to abstain on the referendum vote.

MP Bill Cash's (Con) attempt on 17 June 2008 for a judicial review is rejected by the High Court, which confirms that ratification without a referendum is legal.

The judge rejects the claim on the grounds that it is for Parliament rather than the courts to decide whether the bill should pass, and that Cash is trying to 'pursue a political agenda through the court'.

> **THE BOTTOM LINE**
>
> This means that Parliament's decision to ratify the Treaty back in January stands. On 16 July 2008 the UK is the first country after the Irish 'No' referendum to deposit its instrument of ratification in Rome.

The Lisbon Treaty says that if more than one million citizens from a representative number of member states (15) petition the Commission, then it should consider the request. But it does not have to act. And the petition can only relate to the proper implementation of EU treaties, not to something people might object to in the treaties. In practice, this will have little impact on the workings of the EU. How is anyone going to bring together one million citizens from 15 states?

Article 50

Article 50 is one of 358 clauses in the Lisbon Treaty. Ironically, it was drafted by the Scottish cross-bench peer and former diplomat Lord Kerr of Kinlochard. It outlines the steps a country needs to take in order to leave the EU voluntarily. Invoking Article 50 kick-starts the formal exit process by serving official notice of an intention to leave the EU.

The author of Article 50, that Scottish peer, hadn't originally seen it as necessary and says in November 2016: 'If you stopped paying the bills and you stopped turning up at the meetings, in due course your friends would notice that you seemed to have left.' He did think Article 50 could be useful in the event of a coup: 'I thought that at that point the dictator in question might be so cross that he'd say "right, I'm off" and it would be good to have a procedure under which he could leave.' He makes it sound so easy.

Article 50 states:

1. Any Member State may decide to withdraw from the Union in accordance with its own constitutional requirements.

2. A Member State which decides to withdraw shall notify the European Council of its intention. In light of the guidelines provided by the European Council, the Union shall negotiate and conclude an agreement with that State, setting out the arrangements for its withdrawal, taking account of the framework for its future relationship with the Union. That agreement shall be negotiated in accordance with Article 218(3) of the Treaty on the Functioning of the European Union.

   It shall be concluded on behalf of the Union by the Council, acting by a qualified majority, after obtaining the consent of the European Parliament.

3. The Treaties shall cease to apply to the State in question from the date of entry into force of the withdrawal agreement or, failing that, two years after the notification referred to in paragraph 2, unless the European Council, in agreement with the Member State concerned, unanimously decides to extend this period.

a. For the purposes of paragraphs 2 and 3, the member of the European Council or of the Council representing the withdrawing Member State shall not participate in the discussions of the European Council or Council or in decisions concerning it. A qualified majority shall be defined in accordance with Article 238(3)(b) of the Treaty on the Functioning of the European Union.

b. If a State which has withdrawn from the Union asks to re-join, its request shall be subject to the procedure referred to in Article 49 (which means starting from scratch and re-applying).

The Lisbon Treaty explained

↪   brexitchronicles.co.uk/ec/lte

January 2009 interview with Nigel Farage (UKIP).

↪   brexitchronicles.co.uk/ce/LL

Jeremy Corbyn's statement on the Irish referendum.

↪   brexitchronicles.co.uk/ce/JC

June 2009 - European Parliament elections

To say there is apathy in the UK is an understatement as only 34.3% of the population bother to turn up to vote. The Lib-Dems get 13.3%, the Labour Party gets 15.7% and UKIP gets 16.5% of votes. The Conservatives win with 27.7%.

UKIP has an in-out referendum on UK membership of the EU at the heart of its programme.

In October 2009 Cameron tries to force Gordon Brown to call an election by saying he doesn't have the courage to do it.

↳ brexitchronicles.co.uk/ec/dvg

November 2009 - Cameron: no hope of referendum

In an interview David Cameron says: 'The Lisbon Treaty has now been ratified by every one of the 27 member states of the European Union, and our campaign for a referendum on the Lisbon Treaty is therefore over.'

'Why? Because it is no longer a treaty: it is being incorporated into the law of the European Union. Next week, the new posts that the Lisbon Treaty creates - a President and a Foreign Minister - will be filled.'

Cameron claims the 'betrayal' was the fault of Labour and the Liberal Democrats and promises that such a situation will never happen again. If the Conservatives are elected, he'd change the law so that a referendum must be held before any further powers are passed to the European Union.

'This is not a treaty that Britain wanted or needed,' said Cameron. 'It's a treaty Gordon Brown was so ashamed of he had to sign it in a room all on his own,' he added, in reference to Prime Minister Gordon Brown's notorious late arrival at the treaty signing ceremony in Lisbon the previous year.

The French Government accuses the Conservatives of 'castrating' Britain's position within the EU by adopting an 'autistic' approach that would take Britain off the radar. The angry exchange comes after the Tories hint that if they win the election, they would strengthen British sovereignty and repatriate a series of powers over social and employment legislation.

1 December 2009 - The Treaty of Lisbon becomes law

April 2010 - Lib-Dems offer conditional referendum

In preparation for the general election on 6 May 2010, Nick Clegg the leader of the Liberal Democrats pledges to hold an in-out referendum should there be a 'fundamental change' in the EU's treaty arrangements.

A promise from a party that has never won more than 62 seats is not much of a promise and is hardly likely to come to fruition.

Here's a really interesting election debate with Gordon Brown going head to head with David Cameron and Nick Clegg on 15 April 2010. Not one of the party leaders had led a general election campaign before. The very first question is on immigration policy, which highlights how important this subject is going to be in the coming years.

↳ brexitchronicles.co.uk/fed

May 2010 - Cameron narrowly wins general election

After 13 years of a Labour Government, David Cameron's Conservative party scrapes over the line with just enough seats to form a minority Government. The real winner, and the one holding all the cards, is Nick Clegg (Lib-Dems).

Was Gordon Brown ever really electable against the charismatic David Cameron?

Although the Conservatives win most seats, they are just 20 short of the 326 seats needed to form a Government. This is only the second time since World War II that an election returns a hung parliament.

If Clegg decides to form a coalition with the Labour Party, then Gordon Brown will have another term as Prime Minister. The battle is on as old enemies hold talks over five days.

↳ brexitchronicles.co.uk/ec/GC

CHAPTER SIX

DAVID AND GOLIATH

May 2010 - David Cameron becomes Prime Minister

On 11 May 2010, following Gordon Brown's resignation, David Cameron is forced to form the first coalition Government since World War II. He appoints Nick Clegg, Leader of the Liberal Democrats, as Deputy Prime Minister.

↳ brexitchronicles.co.uk/ue/PM

The youngest UK Prime Minster since the 1810s inherits a country that is nearly bankrupt, again. Remember the famous note to his successor left by Labour's chief secretary to the Treasury?

'Dear Chief Secretary I'm afraid there is no money.'

↳ brexitchronicles.co.uk/eu/IN

David Cameron, born 9 October 1966, was brought up in an upper-middle-class family. This gave him the advantage of attending the same schools as royalty. From Eton College, Berkshire, he went on to the University of Oxford. At Oxford he was a member of a student dining society called the Bullingdon Club where he met and became friends with Boris Johnson. At the age of 18, he took time out to work as a researcher for the Lewes MP Tim Rathbone, which gave him the chance to sit in on debates in the House of Commons.

Cameron joins the Conservative Research Department in September 1988 and works his way up the ranks. He briefs John Major for PMQs and becomes head of the political section. He is pipped at the post for the position of Political Secretary to the Prime Minister but is responsible for briefing John Major before press conferences during the 1992 general election. The success of the campaign speaks for itself. Cameron is Special Adviser to the Chancellor of the Exchequer, Norman Lamont, during Black Wednesday and when the pound leaves the ERM. Cameron has the task of informing the press of Lamont's resignation.

With a growing ambition to step into the political arena Cameron puts his name on the Conservative Central Office list of prospective parliamentary candidates in September 1993. He leaves politics to take a position as Director of Corporate Affairs at Carlton Communications, which produces weekday television among other things but leaves himself open to stand as a candidate should a Conservative seat become available.

For the second time he resigns his job to run for Parliament and wins the seat for Witney, Oxfordshire, to enter the House of Commons for the first time in June 2001, as Tony Blair starts his second term as Prime Minister. Due to his knowledge of the inner workings of Parliament he serves as a member of the Commons Home Affairs Select Committee, a senior position for a newly elected MP. He steadily climbs the ranks of the Conservative Party and announces his candidacy for the leadership position when Michael Howard steps down in 2005.

Aged only 39, and with a little over four years' experience as an MP, he doesn't get much support from colleagues in the House. Cameron is considered the outsider against such seasoned politicians as David Davis, until his speech at the Conservative Party Conference in Blackpool, October 2005.

↳ brexitchronicles.co.uk/ue/PO

In the first ballot David Davis gets 62 votes, Cameron comes second with 56. Liam Fox's 42 and Kenneth Clarke's 38 votes give an indication of where the race is going.

Here are sections of the 2005 debate relating to the EU, between David Cameron and David Davis (who becomes Brexit Secretary in July 2016).

↳ brexitchronicles.co.uk/eu/DD

In the second ballot on 20 October 2005 Cameron gets 90 votes and Davis gets 57. Then it goes to the entire party membership and Cameron gets twice as many votes, which makes him Leader of the Conservative Party (in opposition) on 6 December 2005.

May 2010 - Greece gets €107.3 billion bailout

This is the first in a series of payments in a bailout package.

Greece's national sport is tax evasion, and corruption is rife. Retirement age is 45 and 25% of the population work directly for the Government (10% is the norm elsewhere). The Government refuses to collect taxes from their biggest industry, shipping, or from the biggest land owner with an income of 20 million euros. What a plan! How could it go wrong?

After joining the EEC in 1981 Greece steadily goes bankrupt and hides it well - until the financial debt crisis of 2010 reveals their skulduggery. The Greek Government lied to gain access to the Common Market by falsifying accounts to give the impression that they actually had an economy. Greece never met the criteria for joining the EU nor those required to join the eurozone.

So, what's the penalty for lying to the EU over so many years?

By 2019 Greece has received €310 billion in bailout funds, but the Greek Government refuses to say what they've done with it. One newspaper writes: 'The combined total of Greece's bailouts is bigger than Hong Kong's economy.' Angela Merkel hands over €914 million of German taxpayers' money, but the people of Greece are up in arms when they find out it is a loan and call the Germans Nazis. The people are not broke, the Government is.

THE BOTTOM LINE

Did anyone do the maths?
A simple guide to the Greek bailout:

➢ Bailout money: €310,000,000,000

➢ Population: 10,770,000

➢ Cash per head: €28,783

Angela Merkel is blamed for the tough public spending cuts that follow the bailouts from the EU and IMF.

↳ brexitchronicles.co.uk/GD

Jeremy Corbyn urges Cameron to write off the Greek debt.

↳ brexitchronicles.co.uk/eu/GA

The UK provides direct funds of €6.5 billion (£5 billion) via the EU for two bailouts: €3 billion for Ireland in November 2010; €3.5 billion for Portugal in May 2011.

↳ brexitchronicles.co.uk/eu/IP

September 2010 - Ed Miliband as Labour leader

As all hope of a coalition with the Liberal Democrats is dashed in May 2010, Gordon Brown resigns with immediate effect. The Deputy Leader, Harriet Harman, steps in as caretaker Leader of the Opposition.

On the day Brown stands down, 14 May, Ed Miliband announces his intention to stand for the leadership position, as do Diane Abbott, Ed Balls, Andy Burnham, and Miliband's older brother David. It's a close race between Ed and brother David but on 25 September 2010 Ed Miliband, aged 40, becomes the youngest-ever leader of the Labour party and Leader of the Opposition.

February 2011 - In-out referendum motion fails

Back in November 2010, Parliament debated a European Union bill, introduced by the Conservative Foreign Secretary William Hague, which should have ensured that any amendments to the Lisbon Treaty would be subject to a UK referendum. This stems from the Liberal Democrat Manifesto.

On 1 February 2011 MPs are debating the same bill when Eurosceptic Tory MP Peter Bone tables a motion to trigger a second referendum in the event that the UK public vote 'No' to any treaty change. Mr Bone describes it as a 'binding in-out referendum'.

> **The House rejects the amendment by 295 votes to 26.**
> It seems Parliament is not willing for an in-out vote just yet.

Now, back to the bill. Called The European Union Act 2011 it is passed by the House of Commons on 8 March 2011 by 330 votes to 195 and receives Royal Assent on 19 July 2011.

THE BOTTOM LINE

Any amendment to the Lisbon Treaty will now result in a UK referendum that allows the people to agree to the change, or not.

This demonstrates how little faith the Government has in EU policy makers.

19 July 2011 - Defining day for in-out referendum

The People's Pledge campaign is launched in March 2011 with cross-party support from the start. It is neutral, neither for Remain or Leave, its only aim is to get a binding in-out referendum on whether Britain should stay in the EU.

They give five main reasons why it is time for an in-out referendum on the EU:

1. Nobody under the age of 54 had had a chance to vote on the EU.
2. The EU had now made the majority of laws in the UK.
3. Ministers and parliamentarians making those laws were not accountable to British voters.

4. Payments to the EU from the British taxpayer were rising.
5. The EC is aiming for more powers of economic governance.

The campaign had support from MPs on both sides of the House: Labour MPs like Kelvin Hopkins, Graham Stringer, and Jon Cruddas; Conservative MPs like Anthony O'Neill; the Mayor of London Boris Johnson; and the Deputy Leader of UKIP David Nuttall. Conservative MP John Baron is the group's chair, and Labour MP and former Government Minister Keith Vaz is vice chair. They get some 128,000 registered voters and 87 MPs to sign up to the campaign by 2012.

From small acorns do oak trees grow

In the initial campaign voters sign up online and promise to vote only for MPs who support an in-out referendum. The pledge says: 'I will only vote at the next election for a candidate who publicly promises to support a binding referendum on our EU membership and to vote for it in the House of Commons.'

The campaign then changes tack and begins to organize independent constituency referendums. The first such, in Thurrock, Essex, finds that over 80% are in favour of a referendum, with a turnout of 30%. The People's Pledge communications director Ian McKenzie says the poll comes as no surprise.

↪ brexitchronicles.co.uk/CD

That provides enough motivation to organize a postal ballot in two constituencies in Greater Manchester. It is a full postal ballot under the auspices of the Electoral Reform Services to ensure there's no cheating. Campaigning on the ground in the run-up to July are MPs Graham Stringer, a former Leader of Manchester City Council, and David Nuttall. Voting closes on 19 July 2011. Over 85% of voters in both Cheadle and Hazel Grove vote yes to a referendum in the People's Pledge postal ballot, with a turnout of about 35%.

It is their intention to canvas 100 constituencies for a countrywide consensus, but this never happens. They do use YouGov to poll 2,436 voters nationwide and find that 61% would support a referendum, and only 25% would oppose one. The People's Pledge winds up in 2016.

Noticeably, one politician is refusing to back the call for an EU referendum, Labour Leader Ed Miliband.

March 2011 - Farage takes questions in EU Parliament

Farage begins by talking about democracy and the EU definition of democracy and goes on to talk about financial problems in Portugal and the EU buying up vast amounts of debt.

An interesting question from an Irish MEP, Mr Proinsias De Rossa who had voted against the Irish referendum in 2008, is whether the UK isn't also a union of nations.

↳ brexitchronicles.co.uk/eu/DR

May 2011 - Change the electoral system?

Labour had proposed a referendum on changing the Parliamentary electoral system in their 2010 manifesto. It happens on 5 May 2011 and coincides with many local elections. The public is asked if the Parliamentary voting system should be changed from 'First Past The Post' to 'Alternative Vote' (AV or preferential voting).

In an AV system voters rank candidates in order of preference. If no candidate achieves a majority then votes for the bottom candidate are redistributed according to voter preferences. This repeats until one candidate gets a majority.

The AV system is overwhelmingly rejected by 67.9% of the public, with a turnout of 42%. It is the second UK referendum ever to be held in the UK.

September 2011 - 100,000 sign referendum petition

A petition with 100,000 signatories, calling for an in-out referendum on EU membership, is handed in to No. 10.

David Nuttall MEP throws down the gauntlet and writes a bill to table in Parliament in a few weeks' time. The 100,000 hopefuls who thought their voice counted and could procure change are to have their hopes dashed. Even before the five-hour debate, the result is already decided, as all parties use a three-line whip to force MPs to vote the bill down.

The same week the petition is handed in, some 80 Conservative MPs form the European Conservatives and

Reformists (ECR), whose aim is to discuss steps leading to EU reform as opposed to totally rejecting the EU.

The ECR group becomes a Europarty in the European Parliament (to give the UK more influence) and grows as MEPs from other countries join. By 2019 they have 62 MEPs from 15 countries in their ranks.

October 2011 - Tougher rules on immigration

Between 1997 and 2009, 2.2 million more people settle in Britain than leave. David Cameron wants a cap on non-EU immigration and tougher transitional controls for those coming from EU member states.

↳ brexitchronicles.co.uk/LE

Home Secretary Theresa May is given the task of reforming the rules for illegal immigrants. She says they must be changed and cites the case of an illegal immigrant who was not deported on the grounds that he had a pet cat.

↳ brexitchronicles.co.uk/ID

October 2011 - Commons vote on EU referendum

Prompted by the petition signed by more than 100,000 people, David Nuttall tables a motion for a referendum to give people three options: 1) keep the status quo; 2) leave the EU; or 3) reform the terms of the UK's membership of the EU.

> **The motion fails by 483 votes to 111**

81 Conservatives and 19 Labour MPs defy a three-line whip and vote in favour, but this is still not enough to make an impression on the end result. Sir George Young MP (Con) comments:

↳ brexitchronicles.co.uk/ue/GY

Nov. 2011 - Eurozone financial crisis, an opportunity?

Cameron gives a speech calling for fundamental future reform and allowing powers to 'ebb back' from Brussels to Westminster. As 81 of his MPs had challenged his authority the month before by voting to support a people's referendum, he goes on to say that leaving the EU is not in Britain's best interest.

↳ brexitchronicles.co.uk/ue/OT

Dec. 2011 - Demands for tougher monetary controls

Various reasons are cited for the European debt crisis (eurozone crisis). Mainly, that Mediterranean countries and Ireland had been unable to repay their government debt, in other words, they were technically bankrupt. In principle, countries cannot go bankrupt so the money has to be found to prop up their economies until such time that they can work their way out of debt. Assistance came via the European Central Bank (ECB) and the IMF. But the effects are a rise in unemployment and low growth.

Austerity is called for, which is so unpopular it causes power shifts as governments are voted out in the hope that the next one will put an end to cut backs. The euro is at risk of being devalued so, at the EU Summit on 9 December 2011, Cameron is asked to join a scheme that will help prop up and stabilize the euro. The problem is that they are asking the UK to pour money into a scheme that could end up devaluing the pound. 'What is on offer isn't in Britain's interests,' says Cameron. He then vetoes the treaty!

The Fiscal Stability Treaty sets out mandatory budget controls for eurozone members. Cameron gives a statement:

↪ brexitchronicles.co.uk/NS

The eurozone crisis has meant states who adopted the euro giving up sovereignty in order to stay afloat. Britain needs no such bailout, unlike many EU states.

The European Parliament is displeased by Cameron using his veto and attacks him personally, branding him a coward. Manfred Weber, vice chairman of the European People's Party, is annoyed by Cameron's 'distancing rhetoric' and believes it is ill-advised: 'The country is primarily damaging itself. The British must now decide if they want to be in the EU club or not. ... The game of always wanting to have a say in the debate while also wrecking every compromise is not acceptable in the long run. You can't be a little bit pregnant. ... It must be made clear to Great Britain: Either you want the whole package, or you can leave it alone.'

Nigel Farage says the veto isn't really worth a row of beans:

⤷ brexitchronicles.co.uk/eu/ftt

Farage expresses concerns about a 'financial transaction tax' that would punish London's financial markets.

There are calls to put pressure on the UK by taking a clear political stance. Co-chair of the Green group, Daniel Cohn-Bendit, says, 'Now, Cameron is a coward. We must put pressure on the British and force them, by implementing tough regulations on financial markets, to decide if they want out of the EU or if they want to stay inside.'

Cameron replies:
'Britain must now decide its new place in Europe.'

As the EU refuses to meet Cameron's 'safeguards' he decides to veto the Fiscal Stability Treaty. They simply bypass Britain and amend the Lisbon Treaty anyway. France and Germany write up the new accord. The EU are about to gang up 26 to 1 and leave Cameron isolated. Furthermore, the EU are planning to punish Britain for not supporting the euro in favour of the pound.

---

24 countries sign the treaty without holding a referendum

When it comes to austerity, people are not wholly enthusiastic. For instance, after a treaty imposing austerity as a condition for receiving bailout funds and continued membership, the people of Greece demonstrate, riot, and burn the EU flag. Reason enough not to hold a referendum.

Jan. 2012 - Fiscal treaty to enforce budget discipline

In an effort to resolve the crisis the Fiscal Stability Treaty is drawn up to create a closer fiscal union and to enforce strict budget controls on the 17 eurozone members. This is the treaty Cameron vetoed last December. It is not signed by either the UK or the Czech Republic, neither use the euro. The Fiscal Stability Treaty clearly gives the EU greater powers by allowing the European Court of Justice to monitor compliance and to impose fines on rule-breakers. It also gives the EC more powers to scrutinize national budgets.

↳   brexitchronicles.co.uk/FC

Compared to most other member states Britain has ridden the money crisis rather well. His party and the country are behind him; he only has to use the UK's strong position to his advantage and claw back some of the powers given up to Brussels. Statistics show that since the monetary union (single currency) was launched, unemployment in the 17 eurozone states has risen to its highest level, with an average of 10.7% (UK 7.9%). The EC announces that €82 billion (£69 billion) is available to spend on projects to help reduce unemployment across the eurozone and to promote growth.

Douglas Carswell MP (Con) on 31 January 2012 sums up what many MPs are feeling: 'From now on it's possible for the rest of the euro club to get together to change the rules and there's now absolutely nothing we can do about it.'

↳   brexitchronicles.co.uk/DC

May 2012 - Ireland decides on Fiscal Stability Treaty

On 5 March 2012, 24 European Union leaders sign the European Fiscal Stability Treaty in Brussels. Ireland's Taoiseach (meaning Prime Minister) Mr Enda Kenny signs it, subject to ratification by the electorate in an upcoming referendum.

Ireland, as usual, is bound to hold a referendum, but they employ a trick they used last time. Instead of asking if the people agree with the treaty, or if they want to leave the eurozone, they ask if the Government may amend the Irish Constitution.

Sinn Féin President Gerry Adams calls for a rejection of the treaty in the referendum, citing that by signing it Ireland will be handing over significant new powers to the European Court of Justice and the European Commission. Adams goes on to say that Mr Kenny is allowing these institutions to impose economic policies on democratically elected governments and to impose heavy fines where they believe these policies have not been adhered to.

The Irish Government is forced to remove some of the content from their website as it promotes a Yes vote in the referendum. It's unconstitutional for a government to spend taxpayers' money to favour one side of a referendum debate.

With 955,091 people voting for and 626,907 against the treaty was ratified.

Ireland, 31 May 2012, vote 60.3% in favour, on a turnout of 50%

June 2012 - EU renegotiation becomes necessary

More than 90 Conservative MPs sign a letter from John Baron asking for legislation committing the UK to an EU referendum after the next election. The letter says the law would 'address the lack of public trust' as past promises to hold such a vote never materialized.

↳ brexitchronicles.co.uk/JB

David Cameron makes a clear statement to the House of Commons: 'There are those who argue for an in-out referendum now. I don't agree with that because I don't believe leaving the EU would be best for Britain.'

↳ brexitchronicles.co.uk/RR

Conservative Foreign Secretary William Hague says that he believes most people want a better relationship with Europe and that leaving would have too many disadvantages. He goes on to admit that there are disadvantages to being in the EU and the time to decide about our relationship with Europe is when we know whether we can get that better relationship.

↳ brexitchronicles.co.uk/PC

Liam Fox says that unless there is a rebalancing of relationships within the EU Britain should leave.

↳ brexitchronicles.co.uk/LF

July 2012 - Barroso lashes out at UK MEPs

President of the European Commission José Manuel Barroso tells the European Parliament that he is puzzled by the behaviour of British Conservative MEPs of the ECR group, as they seem to take delight in the difficulties of the eurozone. He's referring to Conservative MEP Martin Callanan, who had repeatedly criticized bank bailouts as wasting taxpayers' money and talked in favour of eurozone exits for some states.

Barroso went on to say that this is not just a eurozone problem but a European one. The British Government has given more money to its banks than any other European state. Since 2008 the UK has committed €82.9 billion to UK banks and a further €40.41 billion in interventions and guarantees - amounting to €158 billion.

Total UK taxpayers' money propping up the financial sector is €281.31 billion.

↪ brexitchronicles.co.uk/eu/BO

Cameron talks about the public being given the opportunity for 'fresh consent', meaning a general election, but he is still not backing any sort of referendum. Back in the House of Commons, MPs keep up the pressure for a referendum.

↪ brexitchronicles.co.uk/DV

September 2012 - Barroso State of the Union speech

EC President José Manuel Barroso gives his State of the Union speech on 12 September 2012. He says Europe needs a new direction, new thinking. Globalization demands more European unity, more European unity demands more integration, more integration demands more democracy, **European democracy**. He recognizes that the EU needs to reform and calls for a debate on major reforms to make the European Union a 'federation of nation states'.

⤷ brexitchronicles.co.uk/eu/fns

Nigel Farage gives a statement on Barroso's State of the Union address. He criticizes Mario Draghi for the bailouts to keep Mediterranean countries tied to the EU, countries that should never have been allowed to join (since they never fulfilled the criteria). He concludes by saying:

'And I think Mr. Barroso, today, the British people hearing you calling for the EU to become a global power, making it absolutely clear that members states must obey, must obey what you tell them whether they are in the relatively wealthy north or the poorer south. I think those comments - this emerging, creeping, euro dictatorship - is something that will repulse millions of British people and the only good news I take from today is, you've helped to bring that referendum just a little bit closer.'

⤷ brexitchronicles.co.uk/ue/eur

Oct. 2012 - European Communities Act 1972 (Repeal)

Conservative MP Douglas Carswell attempts to repeal the European Communities Act 1972, which would take the UK out of the EU and revert to being a member of the former European Economic Community. Carswell admits the bill has little chance of becoming law but feels the option should at least be debated in the House. As expected, it gets nowhere.

 brexitchronicles.co.uk/rap

On its second reading, Douglas Carswell talks to a near-empty House of Commons - demonstrating MP's disrespect for the electorate. This is the first crowdsourced legislation, Carswell explains that more than 5,000 readers of his website decided what Private Member's bill he should propose.

Seven years later this very Act is repealed

On 18 August 2019 the Secretary of State for Exiting the EU, Steve Barclay, signs the commencement order which will repeal the European Communities Act 1972 on exit day, bringing the European Withdrawal Act MPs voted through in September 2018 into force.

> Cameron has been tested to the limit this year as constant pressure to hold a referendum makes him feel pushed into a corner. The euro crisis is a wakeup call for many Tory rebels as Cameron's veto to protect the pound left him isolated.

October 2012 - Government loses EU budget vote

An embarrassing defeat for the coalition Government as MPs demand reductions in the EU budget. They turn down the proposed EU budget for 2014-2020 by 307 votes to 294.

Mark Reckless MP (Con) says voters will find it hard to understand why there are cuts to UK public spending but that the EU is getting a larger budget. He goes on to say that we simply cannot afford an increase from €9.2 billion in one year to €13.6 billion the next.

↳ brexitchronicles.co.uk/BV

Leaving aside the row about the EU budget, The Daily Telegraph reports William Hague's speech: 'If we cannot show that decision-making can flow back to national parliaments then the system will become democratically unsustainable. ... Public disillusionment with the EU in Britain is the deepest it has ever been.'

There is talk about including a proposal in the next Conservative manifesto for the repatriation of powers from the EU back to Westminster. The Fresh Start Group - a moderate Eurosceptic pressure group formed in September 2011 by three Conservative MPs - is certainly looking into it. Any negotiation on reforms to allow powers to 'ebb back' from Brussels to Westminster (as cited in Cameron's speech of November 2011) will require tough negotiators.

Scottish independence referendum deal signed

The Scots wanted home rule long before 1306, when Robert the Bruce was made King of the House of Stuart. Anyway, Cameron signs a deal on 15 October 2012 to allow a single-question referendum on Scottish independence to be held before the end of 2014.

↪ brexitchronicles.co.uk/AS

November 2012 - Farage on Merkel's UK visit

Angela Merkel is to meet David Cameron in London to discuss the EU budget before the summit. Farage has a message he would like her to pass on to him: 'This simply doesn't work any more, it really is time that the United Kingdom left the EU.'

↪ brexitchronicles.co.uk/eu/WI

Farage gives a speech: 'Mr Cameron heads to Brussels tomorrow, I think on "mission impossible". But it is a remarkable debate to think that the European Union is talking about taking another trillion euros from European taxpayers despite the fact that the accounts have not been signed off for 18 years in a row. If this was a company, the directors, or in this case the Commission, would all be in prison.'

↪ brexitchronicles.co.uk/MI

November 2012 - EU summit ends without agreement

Cameron goes to the Brussels summit to negotiate the UK's contribution to the EU budget. In view of the defeat in the House of Commons in October he'll request a freeze - only paying the same amount as the previous year. In the end, Britain and Germany refuse to sign off the €971 billion budget for 2014-2020. The President of the European Council, Herman Van Rompuy, calls it a day, with no deal. They have three months to agree an acceptable offer.

⤷   brexitchronicles.co.uk/BS

December 2012 - EU gets Nobel peace prize

The armaments manufacturer Alfred Nobel invented TNT. He was so upset by how the military used his invention that he created a foundation to award an annual prize to someone who has promoted peace.

The EU wins it for building a 'continent of peace', the first time an institution is awarded a Nobel. It is presented to the heads of the EU's three main institutions: Herman Van Rompuy, President of the European Council; Jose Manuel Barroso, President of the European Commission; and Martin Schulz, President of the European Parliament.

⤷   brexitchronicles.co.uk/eu/npp

December 2012 - Predictions wrong about eurozone

London Mayor Boris Johnson gives a speech explaining that when the UK decided not to join the eurozone (the name given to those who adopted the euro) many large institutions, such as the Confederation of British Industry, and economic thinkers said that London's financial markets would never survive outside the eurozone; that business would all go to Frankfurt. Against all these negative predictions London remains one of the largest financial centres in the world, with 40% of trade being done in euros, and it exports financial services to the tune of £17 billion each year. The dire warnings of doom and gloom were unfounded, while Eurosceptic predictions turned out to be entirely correct. The euro is a ,calamitous project'.

↳ brexitchronicles.co.uk/BJ

The EU took a battering in the eurozone crisis and a new world is emerging. Payments from richer states to the EU are bound to increase as poorer countries still need propping up. There has been unrest in those member states where austerity is hardest and Athens, Paris, and Madrid all experience violent protests.

Cameron dodges and weaves all year, under constant pressure from the Eurosceptics in his own party, voters handing in petitions, and popularity gains by UKIP, led by Nigel Farage who gets lots of air time.

Does the Conservative Party blame David Cameron for not clinching an absolute majority in the last election? Do they see the coalition with the Liberal Democrats as a humiliation?

A flurry of radical Conservative backbenchers have waged a lively debate on Europe for months.

Cameron refuses to even consider a referendum in 2012. He resists it at every turn and only talks about Britain negotiating a new relationship. He is right to question the EC's growing EU budget, and the lack of democracy in the EU executive and EU decision-making.

But what laws and regulations does Cameron want to claw back from the European Union? The German Chancellor, the French President, and all the other European leaders lose patience with him. It seems that Britain wants to pick and choose policies via a long list of opt-outs, while everyone else must accept the lot. Cameron makes his position clear. He thinks Britain should remain in the EU and negotiate a better relationship, but he doesn't say what Britain expects of Europe.

With the next general election two and a half years away, in May 2015, much can happen.

PMQs on 16 January 2013 - Opposition Leader Miliband crosses swords with Cameron on his long-awaited statement on 'Britain and Europe'. There is no mention of an in-out referendum.

 brexitchronicles.co.uk/eu/dcq

CHAPTER SEVEN

CAMERON GETS IT RIGHT

January 2013 - The speech that changes everything

Prime Minister David Cameron gives an earth-shattering speech on Britain and Europe on 23 January 2013 at 8:45 am. It's the defining moment, he's got it right.

Don't get me wrong, not because it causes Brexit, he gets it right because for 38 years the British people have been denied a say in their own destiny, which he now rectifies.

His Britain and Europe speech lasts about 38 minutes. Cameron says he wants to negotiate the UK's relationship with the EU and then give people the 'simple choice' between staying in under those new terms or leaving the EU.

↳   brexitchronicles.co.uk/ue/ewf

PMQs at 12:00 is a heated debate, now that the cat is out of the bag. An in-out referendum is on the table.

↳ brexitchronicles.co.uk/eu/hcq

Bill Cash tables a question: 'My right honourable friend insists on five excellent principles, including democracy based on national parliaments, and he rejects ever closer union. Other member states want to go ahead with more integration and are demanding it.'

'Last year on the Fiscal Treaty they ignored his veto and went ahead irrespective of the rules of the European Union. Will my right honourable friend [Cameron] tell us what will happen if by next spring they insist on going ahead with their own intended proposals and what will he do in response?'

Cameron replies: 'I believe what is going to happen, is that the eurozone countries do need to make changes to the European Union, they are changing the union to fix the currency. That is what the four Presidents' report is about, and it poses quite wide ranging treaty changes. I think this frankly gives us the right to argue that for those countries that are not in the eurozone, and frankly I believe are never going to join the eurozone, that there are changes that we would like, not just for ourselves but for a more open, competitive and flexible Europe. So, there is going to be change in Europe, the eurozone countries do need to make changes but we should not back off from pushing forward our agenda as well.'

February 2013 - UK contribution to EU Budget

A proposed cut of €34.4 billion (£29 billion) over the next seven years is agreed. Payments go up, but not by as much.

↳ brexitchronicles.co.uk/BC

May 2013 - Draft EU referendum bill

A draft bill is published by David Cameron that outlines Conservative plans for renegotiation and promises an in-out vote if they're returned to office in 2015.

↳ brexitchronicles.co.uk/RA

John Baron MP (Con) tables a separate bill on 16 May 2013 to guarantee a referendum by 2017. It is defeated by 277 votes to 130 as 114 Conservative MPs ignore a three-line whip to vote in favour. The bill was doomed before the debate.

July 2013 - EU referendum bill passes second reading

Just two months later, the draft bill drawn up by Cameron is introduced by James Wharton MP (Con). It requires the holding of a referendum on the UK's continued membership of the EU before the end of 2017. The question as set out in the bill is: 'Do you think that the United Kingdom should be a member of the European Union?'

At its second reading on 5 July 2013 it passes by 304 votes to nil. Almost all Labour MPs and all Liberal Democrat MPs abstain.

Nov. 2013 - Referendum bill gets Commons approval

The EU referendum bill tabled by Conservative MP James Wharton passes its final stage in the Commons, despite the efforts of Labour and Liberal Democrat MPs to sabotage it.

↪ brexitchronicles.co.uk/CA

The bill is given a third reading on 29 November 2013 and sent to the House of Lords for consideration in January next year. The bill gets a second reading in January 2014 in the House of Lords but does not become law. It is essentially blocked by the Lords, who describe it as 'economically devastating' and 'biased and vague'.

Speaking outside the chamber, Mr Wharton MP says: 'Labour and the Lib-Dems conspired in the House of Lords to kill this important piece of legislation, doing the bidding of their political masters in the Commons.'

With the bill now dead in the water Prime Minister David Cameron says: 'As Labour and the Lib-Dems have killed the Wharton bill, the one way to guarantee a referendum is to vote Conservative at the next General Election.'

David Cameron says the Conservatives will bring back the bill and use the Parliament Act to force it into law, rather than see the Lords block it again.

March 2014 - Nick Clegg and Nigel Farage TV debate

In the run-up to the European Parliamentary elections, Deputy Prime Minister Nick Clegg and UKIP leader Nigel Farage go head to head in two TV debates to make sense of the biggest question the UK faces this century.

Two sides of the coin are very well presented during two hours of debate as Clegg claims to be the party for Remain and Farage the face of the Leave movement.

Part 1:

↳ brexitchronicles.co.uk/ue/CF

Part 2:

↳ brexitchronicles.co.uk/ue/NN

Here are the highlights from both debates.

↳ brexitchronicles.co.uk/ue/DH

Leader of the Opposition, Ed Miliband announces in an article in the Financial Times that he'll take on the same policy as the Conservatives. Should Labour win the next election, then there will be no further transfer of powers from Westminster to Brussels without a referendum on the UK's continued membership of the EU.

May 2014 - UK European Parliament elections

European Parliament (EP) elections on 22 May 2014 coincide with local elections in England and Northern Ireland.

There are 73 seats up for grabs in the EP for the lucky MEPs who can persuade the public to actually go out and vote. The turnout is only 35.6%, even after the four main parties have spent nearly £8.5 million on campaigning - the money could have been better used elsewhere. It seems to me that there is more engagement in the Eurovision Song Contest than in who will represent Britain's interests in Europe.

The 2014 European elections cost the UK taxpayer £109 million. This money pays for polling stations and venues, mailing out candidate information and polling cards, transport to facilitate counting of votes, and so on.

UKIP and their Leave campaign are, without doubt, the big winners in 2014. They gain 11 seats and take 24 seats in total with 27% of the popular vote. Labour win 20 seats and the Conservatives 19. The Liberal Democrats, who spent £1.5 million on campaigning, win only one seat. Clegg says on his weekly radio show: 'Farage is the leader of the party of "out"; I am the leader of the party of "in".'

Where are Remain voters in this election?

This is a defining moment when the whole Brexit debacle could be put to rest once and for all. A meagre 35.6% turnout, of which 27% vote UKIP. ... **Strike One!**

European Parliament has its own 'parties'

After the UK decides on their 73 MEPs, the wrangling begins as 751 MEPs align themselves with a Europarty that has similar political interests and build alliances within the European Parliament. The party with the most MEPs has most power in Parliament and for a majority a party needs 376 seats/MEPs. The two largest parties are the European People's Party (EPP), with 221 seats, and the Progressive Alliance of Socialists and Democrats (S&D), with 191 seats.

There are eight such Europarties, including smaller ones like Europe of Freedom and Direct Democracy (EFDD) with 48 seats, which UKIP aligns with, and the European Conservatives and Reformists (ECR) with 70 seats, who can definitely count on the Conservatives as they formed this Europarty in September 2011 to break from the EPP.

This is how electing MEPs works:

↳ brexitchronicles.co.uk/ue/epe

As the newly elected MEPs gather in the EU Parliament on 25 May 2014 and begin to pledge allegiance to a party, a screen shows which party is getting the most MEPs in real time. No single Europarty gets a majority, so a grand coalition is formed between the EPP and the S&D.

↳ brexitchronicles.co.uk/eu/eer

How did Jean-Claude Juncker get the job?

When the mandate of Commission President José Manuel Barroso expires in November 2014 (he'd held the seat for ten years), a new President needs to be found.

The President of the EC is the most senior executive official of the EU who leads the Commission in its work of proposing and enforcing EU legislation, implementing policies, and managing the EU budget. It's therefore really important who sits in this driving seat.

New rules laid down in the Lisbon Treaty change how the next Commission President is chosen. Article 17 of the Lisbon Treaty gives Parliament the right to elect the Commission President: 'Taking into account the elections of the European Parliament and after having held the appropriate consultations, the European Council acting by a qualified majority shall propose to the European Parliament a candidate for the president of the Commission. This one candidate shall be elected by the European Parliament by a majority of its members.'

As MEPs begin to align themselves with Europarties, those running for President of the EC are already jockeying for position. There are no candidates from the UK.

Mr Hannes Swoboda, President of the S&D, says to delegates attending the EP that any Commission President must be one for change and not for more of the same.

Line-up from the five main parties

➢ European People's Party (EPP) - Mr Jean-Claude Juncker, a politician since 1984, with many years in high office; Prime Minister of Luxembourg 1995-2013.

➢ Socialists and Democrats (S&D) - Mr Martin Schulz (Germany), had served on his local council and as Mayor; elected as MEP in 1994; President of the European Parliament 2012-2017.

➢ Liberals (ALDE) - Mr Guy Verhofstadt (Belgium), elected as MEP in 2009; made President of the group.

➢ Greens - Ms Ska Keller (Germany), by far the youngest candidate in the race (33-years-old); born in 1981 she is a member of the Green Party Germany and co-President of the Greens/EFA groups in the EP.

➢ European Left - Mr Alexis Tsipras (Greece), stood as MEP in 2014 for the first time; the youngest-ever Prime Minister of Greece from 2015-2019, he negotiated the Greek bailouts.

A debate between the five candidates is televised live across 30 countries in May 2014. Even though the public has no say in who gets the job!

↳ brexitchronicles.co.uk/ue/euc

The most vocal and public adversary to Juncker is definitely David Cameron. Angela Merkel is also against Juncker, but even more against Schulz. And the other three candidates? Well ... ? The candidates offered by the Lib-Dems and the Green party lack experience (great to have on board but not to run the show), and as for Alexis Tsipras becoming the most powerful person in Europe? I shudder to think. So, there are only two big guns in the running (Schulz vs Juncker), making it a two-horse race.

Back in March 2014 Angela Merkel attends the EPP congress in Dublin where they will decide on the candidate to be put forward as potential Commission President. Merkel supports the nomination of Juncker against his opponent, Michel Barnier of France. Her motivation is to stop Schulz, and only Juncker can achieve that. She goes further than just backing Juncker, she lobbies other leaders to support the Luxembourger, believing him to have the better chance of winning in Brussels against Schulz.

Meanwhile, Cameron is getting ready for his 'Stop Juncker' campaign. He says publicly on 17 June that he will 'fight right to the end' against the principle of giving the most powerful job in the EU to the candidate of the strongest party in European Parliament elections (the EPP in this case). Given the QMV principle, Cameron needs allies, which he thinks he has in the Dutch and Swedish Prime Ministers. He is wrong.

The only name on the list who looks increasingly likely to be nominated at the leader's summit in June is Juncker.

 brexitchronicles.co.uk/eu/jcj

EC has first choice

Although Juncker is disliked by Sweden, the Netherlands, and Italy he manages to win their support. For the first time, the nomination of Commission President is put to the European Council for a formal vote: 26 member states vote for Jean-Claude Juncker (EPP); two - UK PM David Cameron and Hungarian PM Viktor Orbán - vote against.

↪ brexitchronicles.co.uk/ue/FA

Has Cameron's actions and the 'Stop Juncker' campaign ruined his chances to negotiate better terms for Britain in the future?

On 2 July 2014, during an EP debate, Farage forecasts that the UK will leave the EU and says to Philippe Lamberts, MEP of the Greens group, 'Don't worry too much about my presence, because in the next five years I won't be here.'

↪ brexitchronicles.co.uk/ue/WW

On 10 July 2014, just before the parliamentary vote, the EFDD group chaired by Nigel Farage puts questions to Jean-Claude Juncker, who could become the most powerful man in Europe if he gets a majority of the votes in the EP the following week.

↪ brexitchronicles.co.uk/ue/PP

> EP elects Jean-Claude Juncker as the only candidate put forward for the position of President of the EC on 15 July 2014, with 422 votes to 307.

November 2014 - Massive tax-avoidance

The real arguments about Juncker's suitability only take place after he gets the job. A review of leaked confidential documents shows that during Juncker's time as Prime Minister of Luxembourg companies channelled hundreds of billions of dollars through Luxembourg, saving billions in taxes. Guy Verhofstadt, Leader of the S&Ds, requests that Juncker come to the European Parliament next week to explain the urgent action they intend to take to fight tax evasion and tax fraud. Juncker cancels his participation at the last moment.

However, the EPP group does not consider that this is 'a personal issue' for Commission President Juncker and expresses trust that, under his leadership, the EU executive will step up efforts to combat tax evasion and tax fraud.

December 2014 - Farage welcomes Juncker

Nigel Farage welcomes 'Team Juncker' to their new positions.

Farage then predicts that Juncker will spend most of his time during the next five years dealing with the Greek debt crisis and with Britain wanting to leave the EU.

↳ brexitchronicles.co.uk/eu/WP

Annual cost of the European Parliament per inhabitant:

Germany	€9.20 per inhabitant/year
United Kingdom	€8.90 per inhabitant/year
France	€8.00 per inhabitant/year
USA	€6.00 per inhabitant/year

All member states contribute, plus America. Do the American people know that they are paying for a parliament in which they have no say? How did the EU wangle that one?

September 2014 - Scottish Independence

With a turnout in the Scottish independence referendum of 84.6% of the Scottish population, 55.3% (2,001,926) vote against independence. The 1,617,989 voters who want to leave will be heard for many years to come. Scotland has been part of the United Kingdom since 1707. The cost to the British taxpayer of the referendum is £15,850,000.

October 2014 - Conservative Party Conference

A very moving speech from David Cameron on 1 October 2014 lays out the Tory party's future plans. He announces a package worth £7 billion in tax cuts by 2020. He warns that a vote for UKIP will let Labour back into power. At the 43-minute mark he talks about migration from within the EU and promises to renegotiate terms with the EU.

Here are excerpts from that speech:

'But we know the bigger issue today is migration from within the EU, immediate access to our welfare system, paying benefits to families back at home, employment agencies signing up people from overseas not recruiting here. Numbers that have increased faster than we in this country wanted and at a level that was too much for our communities and for our labour markets. All of this has to change, and it will be at the very heart of my renegotiation strategy to Europe.'

'Britain, I know you want this sorted so I will go to Brussels, I will not take no for an answer, and when it comes to free movement, I will get what Britain needs and anyone who thinks I can't or won't deliver this I would say judge me by my record.'

'I'm the first Prime Minister to veto a treaty, the first Prime Minister to cut the European budget, and yes, I pulled us out of those European bailout schemes as well. Around that table in Europe they know I say what I mean, and I mean what I say.'

'So, we're going to go in as a country, we're going to get our powers back, we're going to fight for our national interest and yes, we will put it to a referendum, in or out it will be your choice, and let the message go out from this hall: it is only with the Conservatives that you will get that choice.'

↳ brexitchronicles.co.uk/ue/PE

October 2014 - Surprise £1.7 billion EU invoice

Once upon a time in a distant land, far, far away,
the emperor of Airy Fairy town had binged the funds away.
Grizzle, fizzle, bubble, and sizzle who will pay the bill?
Don't despair, I know a place the kingdom over yonder hill.
Sir Dodgy Dave's got loads o' dosh and even money to burn
A facts a fact, they've got the cash, it's more than we can earn.
So, legislation comes to pass, and all the bets are on,
That Cameron's going to knuckle down and simply pay thereon.

It would be funny, if it wasn't true.

Out of the blue the EC sends an invoice to the UK Treasury on Friday 17 October 2014 for a 'top-up' contribution to the value of €2.1 billion (£1.7 billion), demanding payment by Monday 1 December 2014.

This surprise extra EU budget contribution is apparently for recalculated underpayments over the past four years. Contributions are calculated on the basis of gross national income. Britain's economy had done better than expected, the eurozone's worse, so some countries get a bill, others receive a rebate.

In addition to the recalculated budget contributions, they also demand that the UK pay Germany and France €780 million and €1.16 billion respectively in refunds.

The UK is not alone. After receiving a surprise bill for €642 million a senior Dutch official says, 'We were very surprised and have lots of questions'.

Judging by the following graph the UK economy must have been running on steroids. The graph only shows those countries who paid extra or got money back (in euro billions).

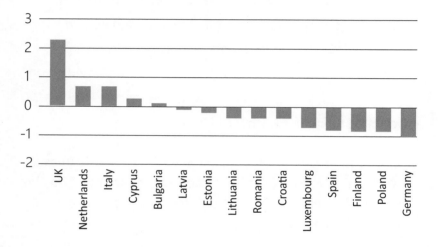

Leaders get wind of these bills while attending an EU summit in Brussels. David Cameron says that 'it is an unacceptable way for this organization (EU) to work - to suddenly present a bill like this for such a vast sum of money, with so little time to pay it. And it is an unacceptable way to treat one of the biggest contributors to the European Union. ... it has never been the case that a two billion euro bill has suddenly been presented. It is not acceptable, and it is an appalling way to behave and I am not paying the bill.'

↳ brexitchronicles.co.uk/ue/BD

The UK tries to negotiate a reduction of the surcharge with European finance ministers arguing that 'the sum cannot be challenged.' Cameron gives a speech to the House of Commons rejecting the surcharge.

↳ brexitchronicles.co.uk/DN

Treasury aides to the Chancellor of the Exchequer, George Osborne, concede that Britain will pay £850 million while not cashing a €1 billion rebate cheque. The bill is paid to the EU in full. The Conservatives claim they've halved the bill, stating that they'd only actually be paying £850 million.

26 October 2014 - EU referendum bill

Conservative backbencher Bob Neill MP again tables a private member's bill for an EU referendum. Before a referendum can take place, it requires legislation from Parliament.

28 October 2014 - Tories accuse Lib-Dems of blocking

Mr Neill accuses coalition partner, the Lib-Dems, of using tricks to block the bill, which fails to progress further.

The duly elected Parliament are still blocking the way, 22 months after Cameron promises an in-out referendum.

> **This is now the sixth time in as many years that an in-out referendum bill has been rejected by Parliament**

November 2014 - Level the playing field

The UK immigration system is dysfunctional and in absolute chaos. With over 2,500 potential migrants in Calais desperately trying to cross the channel, and some 50,000 rejected asylum seekers recently gone AWOL, the Home Office are obviously not coping. Health tourism is a big issue in the press. Failure to implement proper IT systems to track asylum seekers has made the situation even worse. Cases are mounting up, some dating back as far as 2007. Caseworkers dealing with a dysfunctional system are not motivated and morale is low due to the heavy workload, day after day. Farage talks about health tourism.

 brexitchronicles.co.uk/HT

The UK's public conception is that there are millions of migrants and millions of European immigrants milking Britain's benefit system. But the real headache for most people is freedom of movement of labour from Eastern Bloc countries within the EU, which has been going on since 2003. Why would people think like this?

The statistics are:

In 2013, 21,275 children are born to Polish women in the UK.

In 2014 the largest ethnic group in the UK (after Indians) is 790,000 Polish nationals - 1% of the population and more than Irish-born residents. This figure rises to 911,000 by 2016.

The Poles are escaping an economy in a mess and a country rated the 36th most corrupt in the world (World Economic Forum - WEF). But how do you build up the economy of your country when people move out (56 million live outside, 38 million live in Poland)? The people with the gumption to get off their asses and do something have all left.

In 2003 the Czech Republic, Hungary, and Poland didn't meet the criteria for joining the EU but were admitted anyway. Even after the EU invests €862 billion of taxpayers' money into these countries, they still fail to meet those joining criteria.

On the WEF corruption scale the Czech Republic ranks 38th, Hungary ranks 64th. What has happened to the €862 billion?

So, is migration a benefit to developed countries like the UK? During the 1960s boom period it made sense to encourage migrants. Germany, for example sent teams to Yugoslavia to bring back workers, paying for their transport and accommodation. Most migrants send around 20% of their pay packet back to their home country, where it has a higher value due to differences in the cost of living. During normal times, or in a recession, the wages of low-skilled workers get supressed. This puts the most vulnerable people at most risk. They pay little in UK taxes due to low wages and add little to the UK economy because of sending any spare money home. Let's look to the future. Most will probably return to their place of origin for their retirement, being able to live extremely well on a British pension. Again, not spending that money in the UK. I am a migrant myself. I moved to Germany more than 20 years ago and although I have never sent money home, it has given me the opportunity to earn a good wage. Most of the Brits I know here will probably retire to the UK on a German pension, which is at least 25% higher than a UK pension. But I digress.

Germany has a policy that nobody can claim benefits from the state unless they have paid into the system. If you arrive and don't work then you are considered a tourist. Everyone who lives in Germany is registered so the government knows exactly where every single resident is at any one time and it's law to carry ID cards.

It has taken the UK government eleven years to come up with the same policy for the UK to operate on a level playing field with other developed states in the EU. Except that in the UK the press describe it as:

Cameron announces tough new measures

Cameron announces measures to bring the UK in line with other EU nations like Germany. Not so exciting as 'tough new measures', in view of public sentiment of the day. The new measures are:

➤ EU migrants can no longer claim child benefit for dependents living outside the UK.

(2018, Germany sets up an investigation unit when they discovered 50% of all family allowances goes abroad.)

➤ EU migrants must wait four years before claiming in-work benefits, such as tax credits, or getting a council house.

➤ If someone arriving from the EU has not found work within six months, then they will have to leave.

➤ Restricting the right of EU migrants who want to bring non-EU family members into the UK.

➤ Universal Credit is not available to EU jobseekers.

➤ Quicker deportation of convicted criminals.

➤ Longer re-entry bans for beggars and fraudsters removed from the UK.

➤ Migrants from 'new' member states will not be allowed UK entry until their economies have 'converged more closely'.

➤ Extra money for communities with high levels of migrants.

↳ brexitchronicles.co.uk/eu/IC

None of the nine points above were ever tabled for negotiation with the EU. A year later Cameron comes up with a watered-down four-point version not coming close to what is proposed here.

There are more Poles in the UK than from any other Eastern Bloc nation. When 2.6% of your population has moved to the UK and there is a risk of them not receiving child benefits or not being able to send 20% or their earnings back home the Polish Government must act. Mr Rostowski is an MP in Warsaw, Poland, and 800,000 of his constituents live in the UK, they have representation.

Mr Rostowski sees Cameron's speech as discriminatory and threatens that his Government will use its power to veto any plan in the EU. Cameron's proposals would change the Lisbon Treaty and will require an amendment and therefore backing from Brussels to put it in place. Cameron is to present his demands to the President of the European Council, Mr Donald Tusk (who is himself from Poland).

May 2015 - Conservatives win a majority

By winning a majority of just four seats Cameron can lose the shackles of a coalition with the Lib-Dems that had stopped him pursuing an in-out referendum. The referendum was a key issue in the election campaign. Here is another missed opportunity to avoid Brexit. ... **Strike Two!**

The biggest winners though are the SNP, who now have 56 seats, commanding practically the whole of Scotland. The Lib-Dems go from 57 seats to just eight and, as Cameron says, 'they can now hold their party conference in a taxi'.

Labour's Miliband and the Lib-Dems' Nick Clegg resign as party leaders. Farage's resignation is refused by his party and he remains as leader.

Cameron stands outside 10 Downing Street to give the traditional speech immediately after winning an election.

↳ brexitchronicles.co.uk/ue/CC

May 2015 - Queen's Speech includes EU referendum

The Commons are invited to hear the Queen's Speech which lays out her Government's agenda on 27 May 2015.

'Legislation will be introduced to provide for an in-out referendum on membership of the European Union before the end of 2017'

 brexitchronicles.co.uk/ue/QS

➢ On 28 May 2015, the day after the Queen's Speech, Foreign Secretary Philip Hammond introduces the European Union Referendum Act 2015 to the House of Commons.

➢ On 9 June 2015, at its second reading, MPs vote 544 to 53 in favour of the principle of holding a referendum.

➢ On its third reading on 7 September 2015, MPs vote 316 to 53 in favour (281 abstain), the bill becomes law and receives Royal Assent on 15 December 2015.

This is the seventh occasion that an in-out referendum bill is presented to the House of Commons. It passes with ease.

It just goes to show the power of a Queen's Speech!

The Lords and MPs might disrespect the British public but certainly not the Queen

June 2015 - Cameron speaks to EC

This is a defining moment, as Cameron explains to the heads of state the seriousness of recent events. Here are three excerpts.

'I had three clear objectives for this summit: to ensure that there's a comprehensive approach to the migration crisis; to push for faster progress on the Digital Single Market; but most importantly, to get the UK renegotiation underway ...'

'... on renegotiating the UK's relationship with the European Union. The European Union needs to change. Britain's relationship with the European Union needs to change, and I've got a plan to achieve that: reform, renegotiation and referendum. Now we're already making progress on reforming the EU. We've cut the EU budget, we've cut the EU red tape, we're getting on with completing the single market, but this is not enough. We need more substantive reform in four particular areas: sovereignty, fairness, competitiveness and immigration ...'

'... people in Britain rightly think that the EU interferes too much, that too many decisions are taken too far away from them, and that they absolutely are clear about one thing. They and I do not want to be part of an ever-closer union to be dragged into a state called Europe. That may be for others, but it will never be for Britain, and it is time to recognize that specifically.'

↳ brexitchronicles.co.uk/ue/CS

September 2015 - 59.5% for Corbyn

Following the resignation of Ed Miliband there are only two contenders and Jeremy Corbyn is elected Leader of the Labour Party on 12 September 2015. Only four days later he is standing opposite David Cameron in the House at PMQs.

↳ brexitchronicles.co.uk/ue/JL

October 2015 - The campaign groups are launched

Two political strategists start this group, which the Electoral Commission designate as the official organization in favour of leaving the European Union in the 2016 Referendum.

Matthew Elliott and Dominic Cummings bring together MPs from both sides of the House, including such big guns in British politics as Michael Gove, Boris Johnson, Iain Duncan Smith, Liam Fox, and Lord Owen.

A newly formed company, The In Campaign Ltd., is launched and creates the 'Stronger In' campaign. They also have some big guns on board, like Lord Peter Mandelson, Lord Wallace, Lord Wigley, and Baroness Rita Brady. After mass resignations in September 2016 the company changes its name to Open Britain Ltd.

↳ brexitchronicles.co.uk/VL

November 2015 - Four key negotiation points

Speaking at Chatham House, Cameron sets out the four key points that will form the basis of the negotiation with the EU.

↪ brexitchronicles.co.uk/eu/CH

PM David Cameron writes to the President of the European Council, Donald Tusk, saying these four objectives lie at the heart of the UK's renegotiations:

➢ Protection of the single market for Britain and other non-euro countries

➢ Boosting competitiveness by setting a target to reduce the 'burden' of red tape

➢ Exempting Britain from 'ever-closer union' and bolstering national parliaments

➢ Restricting EU migrants' access to in-work benefits.

Former Tory Chancellor Lord Lawson comments that the four goals are 'disappointingly unambitious'.

Cameron may have set the bar low, but he has to get these points accepted by all 27 countries that have a bigger benefit from the status quo. Political correspondent Norman Smith comments.

↪ brexitchronicles.co.uk/RM

December 2015 - Donald Tusk on Cameron's letter

Council President Mr Donald Tusk writes a letter in preparation for a meeting in a week's time. It all looks pretty straightforward until you reach point four, 'the fourth basket':

'The fourth basket on social benefits and the free movement of persons is the most delicate and will require a substantive political debate at our December meeting. While we see good prospects for agreeing on ways to fight abuses and possibly on some reforms related to the export of child benefits, there is presently no consensus on the request that people coming to Britain from the EU must live there and contribute for four years before they qualify for in-work benefits or social housing. This is certainly an issue where we need to hear more from the British Prime Minister and an open debate among ourselves before proceeding further.'

'All in all, it is my assessment that so far we have made good progress. We need some more time to sort out the precise drafting on all of these issues, including the exact legal form the final deal will take. We also have to overcome the substantial political differences that we still have on the issue of social benefits and free movement. The December European Council should address all the political dilemmas related to this process. Based on a substantive political discussion we should be able to prepare a concrete proposal to be finally adopted in February.'

  brexitchronicles.co.uk/TL

December 2015 - PM visits Romania and Poland

Worried about a veto when he presents his proposal to the European Council, Cameron visits the two countries who have expressed they are against his plans because so many of their people migrate to the UK each year.

Cameron and the PM of Poland, Beata Szydlo, give a news conference after their talks.

↳   brexitchronicles.co.uk/pii

Farage highlights migrant problem in Europe:

↳   brexitchronicles.co.uk/eu/MJ

17-18 December 2015 - EC summit in Brussels

Unfortunately, there is no consensus at the summit for Cameron's four-point plan. The main disagreement being the UK's wish to restrict access to benefits for new EU migrants.

   MP Will Straw, executive director of Britain Stronger in Europe, tweets: 'The UK should continue to push for reform in Europe. British PMs have a strong track record of securing EU reform in the past.'

Corbyn says migrants shouldn't need to wait for benefits.

↳   brexitchronicles.co.uk/MP

December 2015 - Lively debate on EU pros and cons

Held at Oxford University; it's time to get informed.
Proposition (Remain) opens with Anne Williamson. Opposition (Leave) Jan Nedvidek. Proposition José Manuel Barroso, former EC President. Opposition Sir William Cash MP. Proposition Nick Clegg MP, former deputy PM. Opposition Nigel Farage MEP leader of the Brexit Party.

↳ brexitchronicles.co.uk/ue/AW

Feb. 2016 - Cameron gets Polish and Danish backing

After the defeat at the December EC summit, he visits Poland again and Denmark. Cameron is making an all-out effort to convince them to stand with him on his proposals. He comes away confident that they will back him when it comes to a vote.

↳ brexitchronicles.co.uk/eu/PD

18-19 February 2016 - Deal struck by EC

Cameron and Tusk come out of the summit triumphant, announcing a legally binding and irreversible deal signed by all 28 leaders. The deal addresses all of Cameron's concerns about remaining in the EU. Tusk says that the decision now lies with the British people. None of this was ever put into UK legislation.

↳ brexitchronicles.co.uk/ue/UK

20 February 2016 - Cameron speaks in front of No. 10

Cameron believes he can create a reformed European Union and announces that the referendum will be held on 23 June 2016. He is using language to scare the public with statements like, 'Those who want to leave Europe cannot tell you if businesses can access Europe's free trade single market'. I hear, if Britain leaves then all trade with the EU will be blocked.

↳   brexitchronicles.co.uk/CS

You don't always get what you want. Or do you?

The date of 23 June 2016 is set for Britain's second referendum concerning the EU in over 40 years. The basis of the referendum is to renegotiate the UK's relationship with the EU and then to give the people the option to remain with a negotiated deal or to leave. Cameron has renegotiated but, for all the bravado, does the deal fall short of what he was asking for? His Chatham House speech laid out in detail what he wanted. After the deal, he feels confident enough to say it is giving the United Kingdom 'special status within the European Union' and he recommends the country vote Remain in four months' time. Let's take a look at the draft proposals.

Economic Governance

There are 'reassurances' that decisions will not be made favouring eurozone members over non-eurozone countries. It goes further in that non-eurozone countries will not be required to contribute to bailouts for eurozone countries.

In view of how easily the EP annulled the Irish referendum, are 'reassurances' really enough? I honestly think that when push comes to shove the EU will protect their own interests first. The phrase Cameron used when the eurozone crisis first hit and bailouts were being prepared was: 'This deal is not in Britain's best interest.' He vetoed the deal, but they simply went over his head and did it anyway.

Competitiveness

In this 'basket' there was a clear statement from the EU: 'The relevant EU institutions and the Member States will make all efforts to strengthen the internal market and to adapt it to keep pace with the changing environment.' This all makes good sense and the EU have been working tirelessly on this issue for many years.

Sovereignty

The proposal said: 'It is recognized that the United Kingdom, in the light of the specific situation it has under the Treaties, is not committed to further political integration into the European Union. The substance of this will be incorporated into the Treaties at the time of their next revision in accordance with the relevant provisions of the Treaties and the respective constitutional requirements of the Member States, so as to make it clear that the references to ever closer union do not apply to the United Kingdom.' Could it be more vague?

A 'red-card' system is proposed that would allow a member of the Council, with the support of 15 other members (there are only 28 in all), to return a recommendation to the European Parliament for further changes to any policy. This is not a veto as MEPs could still go ahead if they believe that they have addressed the concerns raised by the 'red card'. The 'yellow card' already exists and has only ever been used twice; an 'orange card' has never been used.

Social benefits and free movement

Member States, including the UK, could request (only once) an 'emergency brake' to limit access to in-work benefits for new arrivals from another named EU State. In the event a particular EU State experiences a mass exodus of people, a request could be put to the EP for approval, which they have the option to refuse. The emergency brake can be kept in place for a maximum period of seven years.

If, for example, 1.3 million people suddenly arrive in your country, it's too late to put such a plan in place as there is no mention of it being backdated. Also, the 'Visegrád Four' - the Czech Republic, Hungary, Poland and Slovakia – could veto it with QMV. Remember how voting in the Eurovision goes?

Wording will be changed with regard to deportation from 'does' to 'likely to' cause a threat.

No change is made to the principle of claiming child benefit for children residing elsewhere. However, adjustments can be made in the amount paid to reflect the difference in spending power in the country it is to be paid to. This is so vague that any court would overturn it.

In an attempt to curb sham marriages to gain EU access, legislation will be made to limit the ability of a non-EU national to gain the right to live and work in the EU. Any such law will certainly be challenged in the Court of Human Rights and most likely be overturned.

Is it a great deal?

Compared to Cameron's November 2014 list of nine tough new measures (see page 178), his Chatham House speech lists a very watered-down version. Even this 'disappointingly unambitious' version is contested by Tusk. I believe the referendum should never have gone ahead on the basis of this negotiation as it didn't really tick off Cameron's list as made clear during his Chatham House speech. The consensus of opinion agrees.

> ### So, the referendum is now:
> ### Remain on a half-baked deal or Leave.

This is an important point because there are those who will vote Leave anyway, and those who will vote Remain regardless. The undecided will now be tempted to vote Leave. Some with the notion that if the Leave vote wins it will give Cameron leverage to renegotiate an even better deal.

> ### Were the British people properly informed?

May 2016 - Remain flyer sent to every house

The Government had embedded in the European Union Referendum Act 2015 the right to send a 'guide' to every household in the UK and Gibraltar. The leaflet is titled 'Why the Government believes that voting to remain in the European Union is the best decision for the UK' and states: 'This is your decision. The Government will implement what you decide'. This is in the week beginning 16 May 2016, at a cost of £9.3 million to the taxpayer, under the guise that the Government had a public duty to inform.

↳   brexitchronicles.co.uk/GL

Cameron uses taxpayers' money to sway public opinion to vote Remain in a national referendum. It is legal as the House had passed legislation making it so. Why do Leave MPs sign off on this? Because it is presented to Parliament as a 'guide' to inform and not as a propaganda sheet for Remain.

June 2016 - Cameron and Gove Q&A on In or Out?

A one-hour interview with David Cameron on immigration, taxes, tariffs, EU meddling in UK laws, and money - all from a Remain aspect.

↳   brexitchronicles.co.uk/ue/QA

Here's the other side of the coin from another Conservative, Michael Gove on the same issues from a Leave aspect.

↳ brexitchronicles.co.uk/GQ

> **In the week before, ALL polls reckon a majority of 2%-4% for Remain**

Two and a half years have gone by since Cameron's 'Britain and Europe' speech on 23 January 2013 announcing a referendum. It has allowed plenty of time for the public to weigh up all the facts. There are lots of lively debates, and each side spent £7 million on campaigning, on top of the Government's 'informative' flyer. Cameron believes he has negotiated a deal that the public will be happy with.

In the lead-up to the referendum Conservatives, Labour, SNP, and Lib-Dems all root for Remain. The BBC and the majority of UK news media show an obvious bias toward Remain.

> **The cards are stacked in favour of Remain**

I personally thought the question on the referendum ballot was really simple, not at all ambiguous, with no conditions attached but lots of consequences. It made perfect sense.

'A ddylai'r Deyrnas Unedig aros yn aelod o'r Undeb Ewropeaidd neu adael yr Undeb Ewropeaidd?'

The Welsh version was only used in Wales, in the UK it reads:

'Should the United Kingdom remain a member of the European Union or leave the European Union?'

The official Leave group, led by UKIP and such leaders as Johnson, Gove, Fox, Davis, and Rees-Mogg, are clearly the underdogs when it comes to clout. Funds for campaigning are limited to £7 million and a few national newspapers obviously support them. They nevertheless put up a fairly good fight. In my opinion, not such a great campaign and certainly not one that deserves to win.

The then Mayor of London, Boris Johnson, has to do a lot of soul searching in February before deciding which camp he is in, saying it is an 'agonisingly difficult' decision.

 brexitchronicles.co.uk/BH

The British public are enthusiastic though, with reports of some 2.6 million people registering to vote in the final month.

As most people really don't understand what the debacle is about (have you done our EU test?) what are people basing their vote on?

Could it be that personalities and the trustworthiness of the main players are the biggest influences on the result?

Thursday 23 June 2016 - Britain votes In or Out

33,577,342 people out of a potential 46,500,001 vote.

↳ brexitchronicles.co.uk/ue/RN

Leave vote wins by 1,269,528 votes, a lead of 3.78%

There's no point discussing who voted, what age they were, and least of all which social class, after the horse has bolted. An unusually high turnout of 72.2% says public engagement was high. Some explanation for the unexpected end result may lie in the scare tactics of the remain camp backfiring, together with no real solution being offered for the migration problem and the £350 million a week EU payments on the bus. Anyway, **... Strike Three!**

The next day, Cameron gives his final speech and resigns.

↳ brexitchronicles.co.uk/ue/CR

Let's reflect on what happened.

↳ brexitchronicles.co.uk/eu/CW

BO

THE BREXIT
BETRAYAL

(2016 - 2019)

INTRODUCTION

The People Have Spoken

Forty years of successive prime ministers talking about European Union reforms that never happened is probably a major factor in bringing about the 2016 referendum.

So, the people have spoken.

In a democracy that usually counts for something, or it used to. Doesn't the UK pride itself on upholding democracy? I'm therefore embarrassed that I have to define the word to plug a fundamental deficit in the UK education system.

Democracy is a Greek concept (δημοκρατία/dēmokratía) that literally means 'rule by the people'.

Then there's EU Democracy, which is fundamentally different. Yes, there's voting (but not as we know it Jim), for example, there's only one candidate on any ballot paper. You may have noticed that EU Presidents talk a lot about 'European democracy'.

↳ brexitchronicles.co.uk/br/ED

This reminds me of an interview some years back with the President of Egypt, dictator Hosni Mubarak (1981-2011), when he said, 'In Egypt we have democracy, you can either vote for me or not' (only his name appears on the ballot paper). He said this with the absolute conviction that he was giving democracy to Egypt.

We've seen other examples of EU Democracy, such as when the European Parliament (EP) voted not to recognize the result of the Irish referendum in 2008, or when the European Council went over the head of David Cameron to create a situation that was potentially detrimental to Britain during the recent debt crisis. What they are trying to do is legitimize actions that are undemocratic in the true sense of the word.

↪ brexitchronicles.co.uk/ue/eur

Without doubt those who voted Remain felt an incredible sense of loss when the result was announced. After all, the majority of Parliamentarians and the leadership favoured Remain and the polls backed them up. The shock went deep and there had to be a simple explanation for why the country 'got it wrong'.

Some people refuse to respect the 2016 referendum and are desperately trying to find ways to nullify it. This is practising EU Democracy by seeking ways to enforce a legitimate reversal.

Denial

Remainers try to control the narrative by crying out that the Leavers didn't know what they were voting for.

Were you properly informed? You have a responsibility to get yourself informed and not to rely solely on the salesperson. If you can't answer these three simple questions about the EU then I'm sorry, regardless of which camp you're in, your in or out decision was not an informed one.

↳ brexitchronicles.co.uk/3Q

And it is not realistic to say you're voting for the status quo since EU policy is constantly evolving.

Anger

Demanding a second referendum.

To have a second referendum, the first one must be either executed or annulled by legislation in Parliament. Some say that a second referendum would achieve the same result. Would that result then be respected?

Why not make it best out of three when voting for MPs? After all, people are allowed to change their minds - and probably don't know who they're voting for anyway.

It boils down to what Remain MPs are planning

Drag out and frustrate the Brexit process to a point where the general public will agree to anything just to make it go away.

Bargaining

Remember the extension, the extension, and the extension?

Do you remember what the referendum was based on?

Cameron's attempt to negotiate a new deal had failed.

The Leave vote wasn't just saying 'Leave', it was also rejecting the negotiated deal.

Depression

The NHS has already had a conference on the negative mental state of young people due to a long drawn-out Brexit.

Acceptance

It will take some years before many people in Britain reach this stage.

An insight to the EU

The EU is simply an economic club for countries that happen to be located next to one another. They are not our friends; they are more like work colleagues. Each country looks out for its own interests and makes sure it squeezes as much as it can out of the club. EU member states cannot work on a level playing field and, due to their economic differences, probably never will. Richer countries (such as Germany, Britain, and France) all contribute far more to the EU than they will ever get out of it; and poorer countries (such as the Visegrád Four) will need support for many years to come. Then there's Greece, who sees the EU as a never-ending stream of free money. But they pay interest I hear you say. So far this has been paid as part the next tranche of bailout funds so, technically, they have never actually paid any interest.

In the UK, people consider that other EU member states think as we do and have the same economic standards. Sorry, but anyone who has travelled knows this is simply not the case.

One of the biggest differences lies in the state pensions. Here's a chart showing what people get as a percentage of their final salary in EU member states. The UK is in last place, with pensioners receiving just 29% of their last wage, on average.

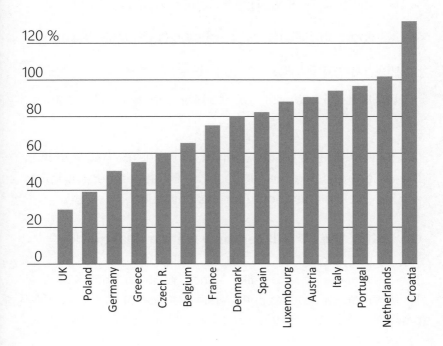

Will the UK lose out on free trade?

Studies on tariffs in the 1960s concluded that import/export duties cost more in administration than they generate in revenues. Today, tariffs are used to protect industries from other countries dumping goods too cheaply - for example, China's cheap steel, which has bankrupted most steel plants in Europe because governments acted too late.

If tariffs were introduced between the UK and the EU, then Britain would receive a net benefit of around £5.6 billion per year, due to the UK importing more than it exports. This could be used to subsidize important sectors.

➢ UK exports in 2018 to EU: £289bn (46% of all UK exports)

➢ UK imports in 2018 from EU: £345bn (54% of all UK imports)

➢ Total trade deficit in 2018 with the EU: -£56bn

➢ The UK has a trade surplus of £44bn with non-EU countries

The EU sells £56 billion worth of goods to the UK more than the UK exports, and the UK pays the EU a membership fee of around £1 billion per month for this privilege.

On tariffs, the EU will certainly want a deal quickly

The EU treated the UK like a rich relative, until Margaret Thatcher put a stop to the unfair practice of excessive CAP payments. Is Britain getting good value for money?

Let's apply some common sense. The £1 billion a month paid to the EU that, among other things, helps Eastern Bloc countries get on their feet (creating a future market for richer EU states) could be spent in the UK. In 2018 a net payment of £15.5 billion in real money, after the rebate, was transferred from the UK to the EU.

Let me put it another way. It's like going to a supermarket and paying £5 at a turnstile for the privilege of shopping there. In addition, this supermarket will say who you can talk to and shop with. If you want to shop next door you must pay the supermarket a percentage of anything you buy there. Read the section on CAP page 24.

Single market access only with freedom of movement?

Access to the EU's single market is already enjoyed by 165 countries, with no requirement for freedom of movement of people. Both Canada (CETA) and Japan have free trade agreements with the EU, without the free movement of people.

Juncker and Tusk state clearly that unless the UK allows freedom of movement of people there will be tariffs on exports to the EU. They often mention the four freedoms (free movement of goods, capital, labour, and services). The EU has no choice but to punish the UK for leaving and believes scare tactics will encourage Britain to stay. They must set an example for other member states who are considering leaving.

↪ brexitchronicles.co.uk/rb/CP

Upon leaving, the minimum wage may be unnecessary. It was a direct response to the influx of EU migrants. Taking back control of borders means the downward pressure on pay for low-skilled jobs will cease and wages for young people could pick up.

I look forward to seeing responsible reporting in the press. A scaremongering, biased media have been making buzz words out of phrases like crashing out and falling off a cliff. When sensationalism is used over a long period it has an effect on the mental wellbeing of many people.

What are the consequences of Brexit on the EU?

The loss of Britain's net contribution (£15.5 billion in 2018) will cause the biggest headache by far as only Germany and France are in a position to help make up the shortfall. But since mid-2018 Germany has shown signs of an economic slowdown. German MEP Hans-Olaf Henkel says that the UK leaving is equivalent to 19 smaller countries leaving.

The UK is the fifth-largest economy in the world and the second-largest in the EU

This fact should never be underestimated when it comes to how important access to the UK market is for the EU, especially for the poorer countries.

Britain is seen as an ally by France and Germany when voting on policy in the EP. After the UK leaves, qualified majority voting

(QMV) puts Germany and France in a weaker position for pushing policy through and there is a risk of the Mediterranean countries or the Eastern Bloc coming together to push through policies that work in their favour.

The risk of other member states deciding to leave and causing a collapse like a house of cards is another worrying factor. There are only a handful of member states whose economy could withstand an exit from the EU.

Brexit is a man-made problem, it is not some meteorite hurtling toward the planet over which we have no control. Where there's a will there's a way. The consequences of a hard Brexit as portrayed by the press, such as trucks queuing for 50 miles outside Dover, do not take into account the other side of the channel.

Poland is the largest beneficiary of EU funds (€105.8bn from 2014 to 2020). This has helped them catch up with the West, achieving 5.0% growth in 2018. There will come a point when people will earn more in Poland than in the UK. The Polish economy can be regarded as stable. It exported about £12.88 billion worth of goods to the UK in 2018, so a blockade at Calais of just four weeks would lose Poland £1,000,000,000 in trade. The economy might be stable, but such a situation could collapse many companies in Poland, with a devastating effect on the Polish economy.

↳ brexitchronicles.co.uk/PL

CHAPTER EIGHT

Brexit Means Brexit

July 2016 - May in charge in under 3 weeks

Theresa May, a Remainer, wins against three experienced Brexit MPs to become the second female British Prime Minister on 13 July 2016. Right from the start she coins the phrase, 'Brexit means Brexit'. She creates a Cabinet in which three-quarters are Remainers.

With 330 seats in Parliament, she thinks she has a good chance of pushing policy through. She immediately assigns the job of Brexit Secretary to David Davis MP, who was Europe Minister. Boris Johnson becomes Foreign Secretary.

Despite a majority in the House of Commons, May finds it impossible to push through any Brexit deal. The problems a mostly Remain House cause her are, I'm sure, in part to blame for Cameron quitting his post. The real problem is highlighted in the maps over the page.

↳ brexitchronicles.co.uk/rb/SM

As we have seen, PM May has a very good hand with which to negotiate a deal with the EU, who has more to lose if the end solution is no-deal. Remember, the world is still hurting from a financial crisis that affected the UK less than most EU states, partly because it was not in the eurozone. Sensible housekeeping by the UK Government and timely reactions from the Bank of England all contribute to the UK doing OK.

Comparing debt to GDP ratios indicates a country's financial standing. In 2016, Germany's debt to GDP ratio was 60.9%, France's 98.4%, Italy's 132.2%, and the UK's 86.8%. Germany therefore has the least amount of debt.

If you remember, in 1979 the UK had a debt to GDP ratio of only 44.55%, which was considered a big problem as interest rates of over 10% were very high. Low interest rates mean cheaper borrowing for governments, so the 2016 ratios are not so problematic, on condition interest rates remain low.

Slovakia, with a debt to GDP ratio of 49%, Romania with 36%, the Czech Republic with 32.75%, and Poland with 49%, all have much less debt than the West. So why is the EU still handing over billions in 'modernization' funds?

If Britain stops paying the one billion pounds per month to the EU it would go a long way to reducing the UK's national debt of more than double that of those 'poor' countries who receive massive EU funding.

HOW CONSTITUENCIES VOTED IN THE 2016 REFERENDUM

HOW MPs VOTED IN THE 2016 REFERENDUM

A comparison of the two maps highlights how many MPs who represent Leave constituencies voted Remain and vice versa.

If the referendum is considered on a constituency basis, which is how we vote for MPs, then the Leave result is really overwhelming, with 406 voting Leave and 242 Remain.

With two-thirds of UK constituencies voting Leave, consider how this might translate in the next general election.

The 2016 referendum (which cost £129 million) is 'advisory', which means that the Government has no obligation whatsoever to act on it. At the Conservative Party Conference on 2 October 2016 PM May announces a repeal of the European Communities Act 1972 and that she will trigger Article 50, as required by the Lisbon Treaty. She goes on to say that she will go for a 'hard' Brexit if that is the only option to end the free movement of people from the EU.

 ↳ brexitchronicles.co.uk/rb/MD

October 2016 - Gina Miller got it right

The millionaire and activist Gina Miller argues in court (R. Miller v Secretary of State for Exiting the European Union) that the Government cannot trigger Article 50 without approval from Parliament and that only Parliament can take away rights that Parliament has granted.

On 3 November 2016 the court rules in her favour that Parliament has to legislate before Article 50 can be triggered.

May's Government appeals directly to the Supreme Court, who deliver their judgement in January 2017, upholding the High Court ruling by a majority of 8-3.

↪ brexitchronicles.co.uk/SC

In effect, Gina Miller has taken an advisory referendum and forced Parliament to make it a legally binding undertaking by the Government to trigger Article 50.

Regardless of how much you may disagree with it, only Parliament is sovereign, and Miller's questioning was right. This is taking back power by allowing our own courts to decide.

When people now ask if it was legal to trigger Article 50, the answer is simply yes, as Parliament created the legislation.

THE BOTTOM LINE

Parliament approves triggering Article 50

The House of Commons votes 498 to 114, and the House of Lords votes 274 to 118 in favour of passing the Brexit bill (Notification of Withdrawal), which becomes law on 16 March 2017.

---

28 October 2016 - The High Court in Northern Ireland rules in favour of the UK Government, saying that they do not require the consent of the Northern Ireland Assembly to leave the EU.

Theresa May statement on EC summit

In October 2016 Theresa May attends her first European Council summit. In a press conference afterwards she says, 'The UK is leaving the EU, but we are not leaving Europe - and we are not turning our backs on our friends and allies.'

'While we have not yet formally started the exit negotiations, here at this summit I have been clear that my aim is to cement Britain as a close partner of the EU once we have left.'

'Yes, the United Kingdom will be a fully independent, sovereign country, free to make our own decisions on a whole host of different issues, such as how we choose to control immigration.'

↳ brexitchronicles.co.uk/OS

November 2016 - PM Szydło at No. 10

PM May meets with the Polish Prime Minister and a statement at the end makes some very important points.

'Since we last met in July, the UK has made significant progress to prepare for the negotiations and I will trigger Article 50 before the end of March next year.'

'I have also reiterated my plan to guarantee the rights of Poles and other Europeans currently living in the UK, so long as the rights of British citizens living across the EU are guaranteed.'

The Polish PM said, 'We want to make sure that as part of the negotiations, the guarantees are maintained for the Polish citizens who live and work in the United Kingdom.'

↪ brexitchronicles.co.uk/br/SB

December 2016 - EU plans leaked

A leaked document reveals the tone of EU negotiations with regard to the UK and how directives from the European Commission are sidestepping the European Parliament. It says: Juncker will act as chief negotiator; a hardline stance will be taken; access to the single market requires acceptance of all four freedoms, which includes the free movement of people.

↪ brexitchronicles.co.uk/rb/PX

January 2017 - Negotiation objectives

Theresa May gives a speech at Lancaster House, where Margaret Thatcher announced her support for a single European market 29 years earlier. May sets out a 12-point plan that amounts to one big goal: a new, positive, and constructive partnership between Britain and the European Union. Her message to the four nations of the United Kingdom is that she wants a smooth and orderly Brexit.

↪ brexitchronicles.co.uk/br/ON

PMQs after the speech

PMQs on 18 January highlight the differences between the political parties as to how Britain will negotiate an exit from the EU, and the problems to come.

↳ brexitchronicles.co.uk/rb/DA

February 2017 - Government White Paper

PM May and her Government publish a White Paper called, 'The United Kingdom's exit from, and new partnership with, the European Union'. It sets out proposals for future legislation and confirms details of the Prime Minister's 12 principles from her speech in January.

Parliament creates legislation so that Theresa May can trigger Article 50 voting 498 to 114. When you look closely at the MPs they're very subdued and not many are cheering.

↳ brexitchronicles.co.uk/rb/ZZ

The EU nominates the Commission as the organization within the union responsible for negotiations and appoints Michel Barnier as chief negotiator. Acting on a mandate from the EU27 leaders, he will negotiate and report back to the Council.

March 2017 - Article 50 Triggered

Parliamentary legislation allows PM May to trigger Article 50. On 29 March 2017 she gives formal notification to the EU in a letter handed to the European Council President, Donald Tusk, by Sir Tim Barrow, the UK's permanent representative in Brussels. There's now no turning back. Once triggered, Article 50 cannot be unilaterally reversed. This marks the beginning of a two-year countdown to leaving.

Tusk, now starting his second term as Council President says, 'I personally wish the UK hadn't chosen to leave the EU, but the majority of British voters decided otherwise. Therefore, we must do everything we can to make the process of divorce the least painful for the EU.' He is obviously personally touched and is practically in tears as he speaks to the press.

 brexitchronicles.co.uk/br/AF

Within 48 hours of receiving formal notification, Tusk issues guidelines for the Brexit talks and calls the European Council (in an EU27 format, without the UK) to a meeting on Saturday 29 April 2017 to adopt his guidelines.

The Tusk guidelines are tough and reinforce the EU policy that a deal to include access to the single market is impossible without acceptance of the four freedoms (free movement of goods, capital, labour, and services). They state that there can be no cherry-picking with regard to the four freedoms.

Here are some of the stipulations in Tusk's guidelines:

1. The European Council welcomes the recognition by the British Government that the four freedoms of the single market are indivisible and that there can be no cherry-picking.

2. In accordance with the principle that nothing is agreed until everything is agreed, individual items cannot be settled separately.

24. After the United Kingdom leaves the Union, no agreement between the EU and the UK will apply to the territory of Gibraltar without an agreement between the Kingdom of Spain and the United Kingdom.

The guide goes on to talk about a single financial settlement, which the press refers to as the divorce bill. It should be pointed out that no actual sum of money is mentioned.

Nigel Farage gives his honest opinion about the guidelines to the EU Parliament.

 brexitchronicles.co.uk/rb/AG

April 2017 - May calls snap election

The PM is faced with a Parliament and a House of Lords that threaten to sabotage every effort she makes toward Brexit. They vow to fight her every step of the way, which creates a deadlock.

She gives an emotional and sombre speech in front of 10 Downing Street: 'The country is coming together but Westminster is not. In recent weeks Labour have threatened to vote against the final agreement we reach with the European Union. The Liberal Democrats have said they want to grind the business of government to a standstill. The Scottish National Party say they will vote against the legislation that formally repeals Britain's membership of the European Union, and unelected members of the House of Lords have vowed to fight us every step of the way.'

↳   brexitchronicles.co.uk/br/SE

The next scheduled general election should take place on 7 May 2020, she has little alternative but to call an early election on 8 June 2017. She believes that a fresh mandate from the British people will strengthen her hand at the negotiating table. The Fixed-term Parliaments Act 2011, introduced by David Cameron's coalition, specifies the conditions under which an election can be called: in the first instance, an election is scheduled for the first Thursday in May of the fifth year that a government has been in office; or when two-thirds of MPs in the House of Commons agree a motion to hold an election; or when a sitting prime minister loses a vote of no confidence and no alternative government is confirmed by the Commons within 14 days.

MPs vote in favour of an early general election by 522 to 13, this fulfils the two-thirds majority condition.

↳   brexitchronicles.co.uk/rb/GE

April 2017 - EU27 discuss negotiation guidelines

The EU27 unanimously endorse the Tusk Draft guidelines on 29 April 2017 just 15 minutes into the meeting. They agree a phased approach, with the first phase focusing on:

➢ guarantee EU and UK citizen's rights

➢ settle the UK's financial obligations to the EU

➢ avoid a hard border between Ireland and Northern Ireland.

At the top of the agenda is protecting the rights of the 3.4 million EU citizens living in the UK. Especially those from Eastern Bloc countries, as the workers' remittances and family allowance payments are crucial to millions of families back home. To this end the guidelines go further and request the right to a UK passport after a continuous residency of five years (Germany requires a residency of seven years).

The EU believes that the UK should make a financial settlement to leave, although UK contributions over the years have helped poorer member states grow, and the UK will never see a return from that investment. The initial figure was around €60 billion but no actual basis is given for how this amount is arrived at.

There will be a financial shortfall to the EU budget when the UK leaves, but richer member states refuse to pay more and poorer states, led by Poland, do not want to receive less. The

UK has signed an obligation to continue payments (circa £1 billion per month) to the EU budget, ending in 2020. The EU has no plans to reduce future spending, despite the projected shortfall.

In view of Ireland's ambitions for Irish reunification, the guidelines refer to the Good Friday Agreement (GFA) 'in all its parts'. In the event that a referendum held in Northern Ireland votes in favor of reunification then they will automatically become part of the EU. There is no suggestion on how to avoid a hard border, and the free movement of goods will continue as is called for in the GFA.

June 2017 - May's minority Government

The election on 8 June 2017 is a disaster and leaves the Conservatives nine seats short of the 326 required to form a majority. Having lost 13 seats PM May must now consider who could form part of a coalition Government.

The biggest winner is Jeremy Corbyn as Labour gain 30 seats across the country, a total of 262.

The SNP campaigned on Scottish independence and on protecting Scotland's interests in the Brexit negotiations. They lose 21 seats, ending up with just 35 - a dozen of those lost seats go to Conservatives. Their commanding majority in the 2015 elections of 56 out of 59 seats in Scotland is short lived. This will make calls for another Scottish referendum less likely.

Back in April the polls showed an enthusiastic 21-point lead in favour of a Conservative win, which is one of the reasons why the PM called the election when she did. The attempt to 'strengthen her hand' and 'secure a Brexit mandate' backfires and results in a hung parliament. The Conservatives win the popular vote by 42.4% to Labour's 40%, with a turnout of 68.8%, although May had dodged debates and was noticeably out of the public eye in the run up. An unpopular social care shake-up the press branded 'the dementia tax', and an underestimation of Labour's resolution to mobilize younger voters with Corbyn's bold promises of ‚free universities', contribute to May losing the majority she'd inherited.

↳ brexitchronicles.co.uk/rb/SL

Theresa May maintains power by joining forces with the Northern Irish Democratic Unionist Party (DUP) led by Arlene Foster, who supports a 'hard' Brexit. They only have ten seats, and a coalition with 327 seats leaves the Conservatives in a weaker position than before the election. A coalition with the DUP changes the dynamics of the Brexit negotiations in view of the complexities of the Irish border and the DUP's hard stance on the EU.

Has this election solved the basic problem Theresa May pointed out when she announced the election? That Parliament are fighting against leaving the EU at all costs.
.... **Strike Four!**

↳ brexitchronicles.co.uk/rb/FG

June 2017 - Withdrawal talks begin

Michel Barnier and UK negotiator David Davis meet face to face for the first formal talks in the European Commission's headquarters on 19 June 2017. They seem very positive on day one that a deal is possible and that it would be far better than no deal. Talks on a withdrawal agreement focus on: 'lifting the uncertainty' for EU citizens living in the UK and Brits living in the EU; a financial settlement; and the issue of the Irish border. There is a separate negotiating team for each issue. Barnier insists that no trade talks can begin until these three issues have been fully addressed.

David Davis resigns and is replaced by Dominic Raab in July 2018; Raab only lasts four months and leaves just before the breakthrough. On 14 November 2018 a 599-page draft withdrawal agreement is presented. On the three issues it states:

➢ rights of those already living in the EU/UK are guaranteed

➢ UK to honour funding to 2020 with a single settlement

➢ the Northern Ireland Protocol avoids a hard border.

↪ brexitchronicles.co.uk/rb/WA

A statement from Siegfried Muresan MEP (Romania EPP group) explains that the EU budget needs to increase to give more money to British universities for research. He fails to understand Farage's explanation that the EU are only returning money Britain paid to the EU in the first place.

The Withdrawal Agreement is endorsed on 25 November 2018 by all 27 member states of the European Council.

An actual figure for a 'divorce bill' is nowhere to be found, although the House of Lords acknowledges that the EU may claim on previous obligations entered into by treaty. Amounts to be submitted for the 'divorce bill' have been estimated as between £30 billion and £200 billion. The Lords report also concludes that in the case of 'no-deal' the UK has no legal obligation to make any 'exit' payments to the EU.

The deal is hailed by Theresa May as the deal that will please everybody - you just know it will end up pleasing nobody.

July 2017 - Cabinet Chequers plan

The EU agrees that the second phase of negotiations can begin, that on future relationships. Differences within the Conservative party on the future of Brexit are to be ironed out on 6 July in a Cabinet meeting at Chequers (the country house used by a sitting Prime Minister). The plan that is supposed to make everybody happy causes the Brexit Secretary, David Davis, and the Foreign Secretary, Boris Johnson, to resign in opposition to it. Boris returns to the backbench. The Chequers plan lays out proposals for future relationships between the UK and the EU, for example, no hard border between Northern Ireland and Ireland. EU negotiator Michel Barnier and EU leaders dismiss the plan as unacceptable. The proposals are never instigated.

June 2018 - European Union (Withdrawal) Act

This bill, introduced by David Davis, repeals the European Communities Act 1972 and additionally requires parliamentary approval for any withdrawal agreement negotiated with the EU. It passes through Parliament on 20 June 2018 and becomes law by Royal Assent on 26 June.

The Act makes ratification of any deal dependent upon the prior enactment of another Act of Parliament which must approve the final terms of withdrawal when negotiations are complete.

On what was to become known as Super Saturday, 19 October 2019, Sir Oliver Letwin relies on this bill to delay a new deal by Boris Johnson until Parliament can pass the necessary law (the deal requires parliamentary approval) to enact the agreement.

December 2018 - May wins vote of no confidence

Parliament has concerns about the Withdrawal Agreement (the Brexit bill). May delays a vote in the House, takes the initiative, and heads off to Brussels to secure further assurances on the Northern Ireland question. Juncker makes it very clear that this is the only deal and that no more negotiations will be held. She comes back with no concessions whatsoever.

On her return, Theresa May receives 48 letters from Tory Brexit hardliners challenging her position as party leader - losing a vote of no confidence can trigger an election. She fights back and wins a ballot by 200 votes to 117.

↳ brexitchronicles.co.uk/br/CV

The Brexit bill, thrice failed, still going strong

On 19 January 2019 Parliament rejects the Withdrawal Agreement by a vote of 432 to 202. Corbyn calls a no-confidence vote for the next day. Tory MPs, worried about an election, rally round and May survives the motion of no confidence by 325 votes to 306.

A month later no fewer than eight Labour MPs resign to form The Independent Group (better known as Change UK), citing Labour as 'institutionally anti-Semitic' and 'complicit in facilitating Brexit'. Two days later they are joined by three Conservative MPs who believe that their party has become hostage to Brexit hardliners.

On 12 March 2019 Parliament rejects the Brexit deal again, with 391 to 242 votes. The leave date is less than three weeks away, but Parliament also votes overwhelmingly to seek a delay to the March 29 deadline. A request for an extension requires the approval of all 27 EU member states. Accordingly, May writes to Donald Tusk on 20 March 2019 requesting the first extension for a period of three months to 30 June 2019. The EU agree a shorter extension to April 12.

Parliamentarians demonstrate how they can waste taxpayers' money and prove they can agree on nothing when it comes to Brexit. MPs take control of the House for three days in a series of 'indicative votes', as each result ends with the Speaker of the House saying, 'the noes have it, the noes have it'. The idea is for Parliament to find some consensus over Brexit. There is none.

On 29 March 2019, UK law makers reject the Brexit deal for a third time, by 344 votes to 286.

THE BOTTTOM LINE

The main question is: Is the deal really unacceptable or will Parliament only sign a deal that ends in a Remain result?

In January 2019 a non-binding amendment to prevent a no-deal Brexit, tabled by Remainer Caroline Spelman (Con), is approved by 318 votes to 310. Following months of death threats, she announces that she will not seek re-election at the next general election.

February 2019 - Free trade agreement with Japan

The Economic Partnership Agreement (EPA) between Japan and the EU comes into force. It gives access to the single market. Can you move to Japan? No. It seems that the four freedoms concept does not apply to the Japanese, meaning they can cherry-pick.

March 2019 - London march to stop Brexit

London voted heavily for Remain in the referendum, which could explain the massive turnout to the Put It To The People march calling for a second referendum. Organizers claim that more than a million people turn up on 23 March.

April 2019 - Time to request another extension

The European Union (Withdrawal) Act 2019 is tabled by Yvette Cooper (Lab) and Sir Oliver Letwin (Con) on 3 April 2019 (Cooper–Letwin bill). The next day it's being debated by the House of Lords in a historically short legislative period. The bill to stop a no-deal Brexit and to force Theresa May to request an extension to at least 22 May 2019 is passed by both Houses in only three working days.

Again, Theresa May formally requests an extension to the exit date of 30 June 2019. EC members question why they should grant an extension that will require Britain to take part in the upcoming European elections and that will continue a state of uncertainty for all concerned. On 11 April 2019 the EC agree to a further extension to allow for the ratification of the Withdrawal Agreement bill (Brexit bill). Such an extension should last no longer than 31 October 2019.

EU members also say that if the UK refuses to take part in the forthcoming EU elections, the extension will cease with immediate effect. The UK remains a full member of the European Union until the day after exit day, now 1 November.

New Exit Date - 31 October 2019

The House of Lords are mostly Remainers and there are attempts to block Brexit by preventing bills from passing through the House. They are warned by Lord Michael Lord.

↳ brexitchronicles.co.uk/rb/PT

Easter Break recess: 11-23 April 2019

May Break recess: 2-7 May 2019

Despite PM May requesting an extension to Article 50 as Parliament has failed to find a consensus, no one in Parliament tables a motion to cancel any of the 17 days of holiday.

Theresa May offers to step down as Prime Minister and to hold a second referendum if Parliament agrees to pass the Brexit bill. Parliament refuses her offer.

7 June 2019 - PM Theresa May resigns

When the answer is still no, Theresa May announces her resignation on 7 June 2019. She will continue as caretaker PM until a successor is chosen.

May 2019 - Theresa May steps down

It has been a tenure of three long years, dominated by Brexit and fighting a, mostly, Remain Parliament. She puts on a brave face to the very end. Her moving resignation speech in front of No. 10 shows her as a compassionate leader with many years of public service to the country she loves. Unfortunately, her legacy will be that she failed to deliver on Brexit.

↪ brexitchronicles.co.uk/rb/TR

MPs are feeling chipper and believe that any old fool can be a prime minister. Ten MPs enter the race for No. 10. Three fail to get the minimum support of eight other MPs (at this stage the minimum to stay in the race) and another quits, that leaves six candidates to battle it out. Two of the hopefuls from the 2016 leadership election, Michael Gove and Andrea Leadsom, throw their hats into the ring again. The final choice is between Boris Johnson (Brexiteer, former Foreign Secretary) and Jeremy Hunt (Remainer, Foreign Secretary). Watch them answering questions from the public to gain an insight into how they really view the Brexit situation.

↳ brexitchronicles.co.uk/rb/HH

When the vote is put to the 160,000 Conservative members, two-thirds vote in favour of Boris Johnson.

Whitsun Break recess: 23 May-4 June 2019

May 2019 - European Parliamentary elections held

This is the election that was not supposed to happen as Britain should already be out of the EU. There's a turnout of only 37% and Farage's newly formed Brexit Party sweeps up, it takes 29 of the 73 seats. The Brexit Party gets 5,248,533 votes against the number two contender, the Lib-Dems, with 3,367,284 votes. A difference of 1,881,249.

↳ brexitchronicles.co.uk/rb/EE

I am dumbfounded and have to ask: Where are the Remainers who love the EU so much that they can't be bothered to get out and vote for their MEP? **... Strike Five!**

CHAPTER NINE

Get Brexit Done

July 2019 - Boris Johnson becomes Prime Minister

The new PM is not elected through a general election but by a postal ballot of the Conservative membership, with 138,800 casting their vote. It's the first time that a Brexiteer is at the helm, and one who was the leading voice of the Leave campaign during the 2016 referendum. The man who's famous for dangling from a zip wire over the river Thames and who sometimes acts the clown, is now entrusted with getting the job done.

The referendum of three years earlier has not just polarized the nation, it's left it suffering from battle fatigue. Can the will of the people finally be carried out on Johnson's watch?

Johnson is a fairly experienced politician who is 55 when he accepts the position he has hankered after for a long time. He unexpectedly ruled himself out of the leadership race in 2016, allowing his friend Michael Gove to carry the torch, who then lost to Theresa May.

Johnson was born in New York to upper-middle-class British parents. His father, Stanley, was employed by the European Commission (his wife's father was President of the European Commission of Human Rights at the time), so the family moved to Brussels in April 1973, where Boris and his three siblings learnt to speak French. Johnson suffered from deafness from an early age, for which he had surgery. He was awarded a King's Scholarship to study at Eton College from 1977 and became close friends with Charles Spencer (Princess Diana's brother). He received another scholarship to study Classics at Oxford University in late 1983.

Johnson's first real job is as a trainee at The Times newspaper, where he becomes a journalist, only to be sacked after falsely claiming that a certain quote came from his own godfather. Through a personal connection, he moves on to become a writer at the Daily Telegraph - it is said that Margaret Thatcher became a fan of his articles.

He decides on a career change and is elected Conservative MP for Henley following Michael Heseltine's retirement. He enters the House of Commons for the first time in 2001. He is already friends with Michael Gove, George Osborne, and David Cameron – his becoming an MP brings them closer.

In May 2008 he is elected Mayor of London. He holds the office for eight years before returning to the House of Commons in July 2016 as Foreign Secretary under Theresa May.

Three years later Boris Johnson wins the leadership election to inherit a party and a country deeply divided over the future.

In his opening speech on 24 July 2019, in front of No. 10's famous black front door, PM Boris Johnson pledges that Britain will leave the EU on 31 October 2019, no ifs, no buts.

↪ brexitchronicles.co.uk/rb/TN

Johnson sets off for talks with the German Chancellor, Angela Merkel. She appears to set him a deadline of 30 days to find an alternative to the Irish backstop. The signs to date indicate that the deal on the table is the only deal, but Johnson seems to be testing the ground to see how much scope there is for a renegotiation.

Next day he's with the French President, Emmanuel Macron, who describes the Irish backstop as 'indispensable'.

If Boris wants to reopen negotiations, he needs the support of the two most powerful nations within the EU. There is a saying that when Merkel speaks, others listen. When Xi Jinping visits Europe in March 2019, who does he see? Italian Giuseppe Conte then Juncker, then Macron and Merkel, but not Sebastian Kurz, Mateusz Morawiecki, nor Pedro Sánchez. EU power lies clearly with Germany and France.

25 July 2019, Johnson's first House of Commons statement and taking questions from MPs about his vision of Brexit.

↪ brexitchronicles.co.uk/rb/FS

With Boris Johnson at the helm, the chances of a no-deal Brexit have been raised and, as the majority of MPs are opposed to this, they start plotting ways to stop such a scenario. Boris seems resolute about coming out on 31 October, 'with or without a deal' - a phrase he repeats many times.

BBC presenter Gary Robertson first coins the phrase 'crashing out' if there is no deal. Other derogatory phrases used by a biased press to scare the public are 'cliff edge', 'hard Brexit', and 'Regrexit'.

What if there is no deal?

Will there be food in the shops?

Only 28% of the UK's food requirements come from the EU. There's a wealth of partners eager to step in and feed the UK – and they are cheaper. The Commonwealth is alive and well and wants to do business with the UK.

All agreements between the UK and the EU have one thing in common, Juncker says, 'EU countries will not suffer due to Brexit'. Juncker might not care whether the UK starves but he must ensure that nothing detrimental happens to businesses in the EU. Will Juncker hinder Spain from selling their cucumbers? Will France let truckloads of goods pile up at Calais and block them from entering the UK? Common sense will prevail, and the Withdrawal Agreement is only about 'divorce' and not about the future relationship between the UK and the EU (which will take another few years of negotiations to complete).

Let's cut to the chase. We're talking about two economies trading in billions of pounds of business every single day. A no-deal scenario would motivate the EU to conclude a trade deal much more quickly and make them more likely to grant concessions. In reality, a no-deal would make the EU agree to a freeze and allow everything to continue until future treaties are negotiated (a transition period).

The EU want to fly their airplanes to the UK, and they want to sell their cars and services to the UK. After all, the UK is the EU's second-largest export market for goods, amounting to 18% of their total exports. This makes the UK not just important to the EU but also invaluable and indispensable – and this is why they're sad. Unfortunately, the biased British press only picture one side of the story, making the public believe that the EU holds all the cards and that food shortages will be the result of leaving.

Some food for thought

In 2017 the EU exports goods worth €375,826 billion to the USA - this includes goods worth €48 billion from the UK.

Top UK export products sold to the USA are:
vehicles ($11 billion), machinery ($9.3 billion), special other ($5.3 billion), pharmaceutical ($5.0 billion), and fuels ($4.3 billion).

In 2017 the EU exports goods worth €259,000 billion to the UK. This represents one billion euros per working day! Do they really want to mess that up?

August 2019 - Corbyn's coup attempt

The majority of MPs are opposed to Brexit and are working very hard to stop it. They shudder at the very thought of a no-deal Brexit. Most MPs now openly say that they will fight against a no-deal Brexit. MPs are aware of public sentiment that a fight against a no-deal sounds legitimate, but in actual fact it is a tactic to frustrate the Brexit process and to pursue their main objective of stopping it all together.

Corbyn reaches out to other party leaders and to opposition MPs with a letter on 14 August 2019 that asks them to support him as a 'caretaker Prime Minister' to block a no-deal scenario. The Conservative minority Government can be unseated if other parties form a coalition with Corbyn as leader.

Corbyn writes, 'Following a successful vote of no confidence in the Government, I would then, as Leader of the Opposition, seek the confidence of the House for a strictly time-limited, temporary Government with the aim of calling a general election, and securing the necessary extensions of Article 50 to do so.'

'In that general election, Labour will be committed to a public vote on the terms of leaving the European Union, including an option to Remain.'

Corbyn's letter is sent to: Ian Blackford, SNP Leader; Jo Swinson, Leader of the Lib-Dems; Liz Saville Roberts, Plaid Cymru Leader; Caroline Lucas MP; Dominic Grieve MP; Sir Oliver Letwin MP; Nick Boles MP; and Caroline Spelman MP.

The letter fails to specify the length of a 'time-limited' government. He doesn't get much support, but it doesn't fall on deaf ears either.

Jo Swinson (Lib-Dems) is up for the plot but is not convinced that Corbyn could bring the other parties together. She suggests Conservative MP Kenneth Clarke for the caretaker role.

It is defnitely treacherous for Conservative MPs to overthrow 'a genuine government of unity' and install 'a Labour government supported by other parties'.

Conservative Remainer MPs Sir Oliver Letwin, Dominic Grieve, and Caroline Spelman only agree to meet 'to discuss the different ways' parties might work together to avoid no-deal.

In an interview Corbyn says, 'A caretaker government should be led by Labour' going on to say, 'We, the Labour Party, by far the largest opposition party, have, I think, a responsibility to take over, to ensure there is no cliff-edge Brexit.'

Nicholas Boles MP, a Remainer, had resigned his (Con) party whip in April 2019 because his party refused to compromise on Brexit. His bill, the Common Market 2.0 proposal, failed at 261-282 votes. Despite the Chief Whip declaring it a 'free vote', the whips had successfully persuaded MPs to abstain.

Boles replies to Corbyn's letter by highlighting four issues that are dividing MPs opposed to a no-deal Brexit. This is a direct response to Corbyn's attempt to halt the 'chaos and dislocation of Boris Johnson's no-deal Brexit'.

Boles writes, 'I do not believe that this proposal is workable. I, for one, will not support a vote of no confidence while the Johnson Government continues to pursue a Brexit deal that might deliver an orderly exit from the EU. Nor would I be able to support any government in which you were Prime Minister, however temporary its mandate.'

'Several other MPs sitting on the Opposition benches have said the same. I therefore urge you and the leaders of the other opposition parties to focus on legislative measures to stop No-Deal Brexit on 31 October.'

Boles goes on to say that the only way to succeed is to frustrate Johnson's plans.

↪ brexitchronicles.co.uk/BX

Corbyn fails to get enough support for his plot, leaving the cross-party alliance of MPs in disarray.

Sir Oliver Letwin says in a BBC radio interview, 'I don't think it's at all likely that a majority would be formed for (Corbyn's proposal), and I personally wouldn't want to vote for it. I wouldn't be able to support that, no. ... You can't just say, "I don't want to have a no-deal exit" – you also have to say, "what do I want to have" and get agreement on that.'

Does Boris have a mandate for a no-deal Brexit?

Philip Hammond (Ind), Guto Bebb (Con), and David Gauke (Ind) all say, 'There's no mandate for a no-deal Brexit.'

Let's analyse the referendum question.

> ### 'Should the United Kingdom remain a member of the European Union or leave the European Union?'

It is a question without conditions. It does not say 'remain on newly negotiated terms' or 'leave with a deal'. A negotiated deal to leave is a conditional deal that contravenes the answer to the question on the ballot. The Government clearly has a mandate for a no-deal Brexit.

August 2019 - Johnson asks Queen to prorogue

Summer recess begins on Thursday 25 July and the next sitting of the House is on Tuesday 3 September 2019 at 2:30 pm. Despite the 'crisis' MPs are talking about, they certainly don't want to miss out on their five weeks of well-deserved holiday.
If Labour want to table a vote of no confidence to kick off Corbyn's coup then it has to be done now. Due to a lack of support Corbyn doesn't go through with it. Five weeks later;

Parliamentarians are refreshed and raring to go. After all, the country is in a bit of a pickle and about to crash out of the EU, go over a cliff edge and into the abyss. One might even say, it's an existential crisis and time one pulled one's finger out.

So, back to work on 3 September, just in time to enjoy the annual party conference season, which normally starts in mid-September, when the House of Commons is declared in recess again. The plan is for Parliament to recess from 13 September–8 October 2019. Conferences are booked a year in advance and there's no return of your deposit on the hall if there's a no show. Keynote speakers aren't paid but attenders pay for their tickets, so it's an important event to raise funds for party coffers, and for the whole membership to be involved in policy making.

Parliament takes a conference recess every year

As a comparison, the conference recess in 2018 was 13 September-9 October, and in 2017 it was 14 September-9 October.

Which party conferences took place?

All the party conferences took place in 2019. MPs voted successfully to block a recess to stop the Tory Party conference. The parties have always agreed not to have Parliamentary sittings so that they could all attend their respective conferences.

14-17 September 2019 - Lib-Dems in Bournemouth, England

20-21 September - UKIP in Caerleon, Wales

21-25 September 2019 - Labour in Brighton, England

4-6 October - Green Party in Newport, Wales.

13-15 October – SNP in Aberdeen, Scotland

Parliamentary sessions normally last one year. Due to the Brexit crisis, the current Parliamentary session has been ongoing since 13 June 2017, as directed by the Government. They have been in session for over two years.

As the newly elected Prime Minister, Johnson claims he needs time to hammer out plans for the country's future and to prepare the Queen's Speech that sets out his legislative agenda for the opening of a new Parliament in October.

On 28 August 2019, Boris asks Queen Elizabeth II to prorogue parliament between 9 and 12 September. This amounts to four more days before the conference recess.

The Queen gives her consent

↪ brexitchronicles.co.uk/br/GP

An interview with Sir John Redwood MP (Con) and Layla Moran MP (Lib-Dems) on 28 August highlights the difference in opinions during this time. Moran says proroguing is to avoid scrutiny of Johnson's Brexit plans. After a five-week holiday, she emphatically says they should cancel all party conferences to sit in Parliament and debate Brexit (no party conferences have ever been cancelled.)

Redwood says, 'We are following precedent, we always have three weeks off for the party conferences and then we usually have a short gap at the end of each parliamentary year, now the previous government decides to go for the biggest ever, long session, it is high time we had a new Queen's Speech and a full debate about the direction of the Government with a new Prime Minister. I'm looking forward to that Queen's Speech and I would recommend Opposition MPs join in that debate.'

Moran replies, 'I WANT TO WORK. It is utterly ridiculous that at a time of crisis, if you were in any other job and your organization was going through a crisis, let alone the country, us, as parliamentarians should be able to do our jobs, you're absolutely right, five weeks, Parliament has never been progued for five weeks before. And actually, I would argue why on earth would we have a conference recess at this time.'

The compère cuts her off with, 'But we have the conference season anyway.'

Moran replies, 'Well we shouldn't.'

(Once again, the Lib-Dems and all other parties have never even considered cancelling a conference!)

Compère, 'But we have the conference season anyway, I mean, you've got four fewer days to do the business that you want to do than you would have done without this, surely if you get your act together you can do the things you want to do.'

Moran, 'People are scared, and no-deal Brexit has real consequences, particularly for the most vulnerable, we're talking about food shortages, medicine shortages, this is the Government that has said this, the same Government that is proroguing us. ... Boris Johnson is basically a coward; he doesn't want to face us parliamentarians, he is stopping the people through their representatives from having their voice and this must be stopped, and it will be stopped.'

Compère, 'And if Prime Minister Jeremy Corbyn can stop a no-deal are you OK with that?'

Moran, 'We, everyone, is pulling together to make sure that no-deal will not happen.'

I must admit, Johnson never struck me as someone to shy away from conflict. The worst thing of all during this time is how MPs behave, they make the public believe that there has never been a recess during September/October. The behaviour of Remain MPs is tantamount to inciting a riot by creating an angry response from the public to a mere four-day extension to the annual party conference season.

Jeremy Corbyn and Liberal Democrat leader Jo Swinson demand an intervention from the Queen. She declines.

3 September 2019 - First day after summer recess

Back from their five-week holiday and MPs are up in arms about losing four days in Parliament.

THE BOTTOM LINE

If it is so important to debate Brexit in Parliament, why has no MP tabled a motion to shorten the five-week vacation time?

Corbyn's plot to thwart a 'no-deal' Brexit starts Tuesday (3 September), Sir Oliver Letwin (Con) tables a motion to take control of the parliamentary agenda on Wednesday.

The House of Commons passes Letwin's motion by 328 votes in favour to 301 against, a majority of 27.

Corbyn says: 'Suspending Parliament is not acceptable, it is not on. What the Prime Minister is doing is a smash and grab on our democracy to force through a no-deal.'

Philip Hammond leads 21 Tory rebel MPs in defying a three-line whip to help vote down the motion – they lose the whip for abstaining. The rebel's include nine former high-ranking Cabinet ministers, like Ken Clarke. The irony is that, with a majority of 27, the motion will pass whether they vote or not. This kamikaze action by 21, strong Tory Remain MPs achieves nothing except getting them the sack.

Phillip Lee (Con) defects to the Lib-Dems by walking across the floor to join them in a symbolic act of protest.

The sacking of 21 MPs is not a decision taken lightly as the Conservatives now have only 305 seats, this leaves them 21 short of a majority, which requires 326 seats.

Boris confirms that the sacking was necessary as you can't have your own MPs handing over the power of Government to the Opposition.

↳ brexitchronicles.co.uk/rb/HC

4 September 2019 - Second day after summer recess

MPs in a cross-party alliance take control of the agenda in the House and pass a bill to force an extension if MPs do not approve the deal stopping a no-deal Brexit.

Johnson warns that he will seek an early election if MPs rule out a no-deal Brexit. Corbyn replies that he will only agree to an election when a no-deal Brexit is ruled out. Corbyn's stance has support from the other parties.

Johnson takes his first PMQs since announcing the prorogation of Parliament, after which Hilary Benn's 'Benn' bill, is debated. This is the European Union (Withdrawal) (No. 2) bill, dubbed by Johnson as the 'surrender bill' because he believes it takes away leverage from the UK's negotiating position with the EU. It passes on its third reading in the House of Commons, 327 votes to 299.

Johnson's motion for a snap election is voted down by 298 - 65.

↳   brexitchronicles.co.uk/br/BA

Johnson makes his famous remark, 'I would rather be "dead in a ditch" than ask the EU for a further Brexit delay.'

6 September 2019 - Benn bill passed by Lords

In closing the debate, Brexit Minister Lord Martin Callanan says, 'the "Benn" Act undermines the Government's efforts to negotiate a withdrawal agreement.'

The legislation is presented for Royal Assent and becomes law on 9 September.

9 September 2019 - Parliament prorogued

John Bercow, who has been Speaker of the House since June 2009, announces his resignation. He will leave his post before the House resumes after the next general election.

PM Johnson makes one last attempt to get support for a general election by tabling a motion. With 293 votes in favour, 46 against, and 303 abstaining, it fails to get the two-thirds majority of 434 votes Johnson needs.

Parliament is prorogued just before 02:00 BST on the morning of Wednesday 10 September, to reopen on 14 October. The Conservatives leave the House; other parties stay behind as a protest against Johnson's action.

↳ brexitchronicles.co.uk/rb/PS

Let the court cases begin and British justice be served

Gina Miller, backed by former PM John Major, loses a bid to reverse Johnson's decision to prorogue Parliament for five weeks. The Lord Chief Justice, Lord Burnett, says, ‚We have concluded that, whilst we should grant permission to apply for judicial review, the claim must be dismissed.'

Miller's claim that Johnson's advice to the Queen is an ‚unlawful abuse of power' is confirmed by the Supreme Court.

Their ruling in her favour states, 'It did not need to look at the motive of prorogation, but that what mattered was the effect of prorogation.'

The Supreme Court reached its judgement unanimously on 24 September and found that proroguing for five weeks was unlawful. Parliament is to resume on 25 September 2019.

Separately, the Court of Session in Edinburgh rules that Johnson's Parliament shutdown is unlawful. However, this ruling has no consequences as Scottish courts have no jurisdiction over the UK Parliament.

In the meantime, the Lib-Dems, UKIP, and Labour are enjoying their party conferences - until the news comes that they must return to Westminster on 25 September at 11:30 am. Boris Johnson is attending the UN General Assembly in New York and cuts his visit short.

25 September 2019 - Day 1 after court ruling

John Bercow addresses the returned MPs, 'Colleagues, welcome back to our place of work. The UK Supreme Court ruled yesterday that Parliament has not been prorogued and that the Speaker of the House of Commons and the Lords' Speaker can take immediate steps to enable each house to meet as soon as possible to decide upon a way forward.'

The Attorney General, the Rt Hon Geoffrey Cox, gives a statement on the prorogation of Parliament and takes questions from MPs as he tries to justify the Government's position.

Boris Johnson asks Corbyn to call the general election that he'd agreed to once the Benn Act became law. Why won't he do this? He invites Corbyn to call a motion of no confidence to trigger an election. Corbyn deflects and declines to do it. No legislation is made this Wednesday, just a lot of ranting.

↳ brexitchronicles.co.uk/br/PR

26 September 2019 - Day 2 - Not much done today

John Bercow begins by reprimanding MPs for their dreadful behaviour in the House the previous day, 'There was an atmosphere in the chamber worse than any I've known in my 22 years in the House. On both sides, passions were inflamed, angry words were uttered, the culture was toxic.'

A motion is tabled to adjourn parliament for one week to allow Tory politicians to attend their party conference in Manchester. It is voted down by 306 votes to 289. Eight Tory MPs have the whip removed for voting against the motion.

MPs' hue and cry over previous weeks about their right to debate in Parliament during this time of crisis is already losing momentum. By 4:00 pm, fewer than 50 MPs out of a possible 650 are attending debates. Obviously, enthusiasm is waning by day two. Steve Baker (Con) talks to a near-empty House about the similarities between the abandoned EU Constitution and the Lisbon Treaty.

↳ brexitchronicles.co.uk/rb/RR

September 29-October 2 - Tory party conference

Conservatives get-together under the motto 'Get Brexit Done'.

3 October 2019 - Parliament negotiation update

Boris updates Parliament on the current state of play in the negotiations with the EU. He announces the replacement of the backstop, preventing a hard border between Northern Ireland and the Republic of Ireland. After which, once again MPs speak to a near-empty house. I thought Layla Moran MP and her Lib-Dems colleagues were eager to get back to work? Alas, they are nowhere to be seen.

⤷ brexitchronicles.co.uk/br/TC

14 October 2019 - Queen's Speech opens Parliament

⤷ brexitchronicles.co.uk/rb/ES

17 October 2019 - 'We have a deal'

When the EU Commission President Jean-Claude Juncker announces that 'We have a deal' there should be a sigh of relief among all MPs back in Blighty as all that effort to avoid a no-deal has paid off because 'We have a deal!'. Boris calls it a great new deal that takes back control. Even before they have seen it, the deal is immediately rejected by Arlene Foster, Leader of the DUP, and by the Labour leader Jeremy Corbyn.

⤷ brexitchronicles.co.uk/rb/JS

19 October 2019 - Super Saturday - the House votes

The substance of Johnson's deal is not much different from Theresa May's deal, which was turned down by Parliament three times. The main change is the way Northern Ireland's border with Ireland is dealt with. It allows NI to remain part of the UK, and the free movement of goods into Ireland. Some MPs are already claiming that it is worse than the old deal. Worse being a relative term, because a deal that might be acceptable to the House of Commons has got to be a worse deal in the eyes of Remainers.

To kick the day off, Sir Oliver Letwin (Ind) - one of the 21 Conservative MPs who lost the whip back in September - tables the 'Letwin Amendment', which passes by 322 votes to 306. This amendment ties Johnson's hands and forces him to request an extension via the Benn Act, regardless of whether Parliament votes the deal through this day or not. This has got to be one of the cleverest smash and grabs on our democracy to frustrate a bill that I have seen. The European Union (Withdrawal) Act 2018 makes ratification of any deal dependent upon prior enactment of another Act of Parliament to approve the final terms of the deal. Approval for Boris Johnson's deal is therefore withheld until Parliament passes the necessary law to enact the agreement.

↳ brexitchronicles.co.uk/SS

The Government then cancels the main vote, which was to approve the deal. Scheduling a 'meaningful vote' on the

Withdrawal Agreement bill (WAB) for the coming Tuesday (22 October). With only 297 Conservative MPs, the numbers are dwindling - so many have either left or had the whip withdrawn.

Boris requests Article 50 extension

A letter requesting an extension for Article 50 to 31 January 2020 is sent to Tusk, as required by the Benn Act. A second letter from Boris to Tusk explains the events of the day and his commitment to seek ratification of the deal next week.

Corbyn's war cry - Deal threatens workers' rights

The withdrawal deal is only concerned with three points, as we've already discussed. Workers' rights are certainly not one of those points. That is a matter for Parliament to decide on after Brexit has happened and is certainly nothing to do with leaving the EU. True, there are EU regulations that cover workers' rights, and I would expect any future Labour party to ensure those rights are protected, but to suggest that it should be part of a withdrawal agreement is simply making trouble unnecessarily. According to the Withdrawal Agreement, EU legislation will be carried over into UK law. The reason being, there is so much of it, picking it apart to weed out the bits that nobody likes will take the next 40 years.

21 October 2019 - Speaker refuses vote on WAB

↳ brexitchronicles.co.uk/br/JA

22 October 2019 - WAB passed by the House

The Withdrawal Agreement bill passes its second reading in the House with 329 votes in favour, 299 against. As MPs turn down a fast-track timetable of just three days to debate it by 322 votes to 308, Johnson pauses the WAB.

A monumental moment, as this is the stage when Theresa May's deal failed three times; on the other hand only a fast-track timetable will achieve an exit on 31 October, as promised by Boris.

↳ brexitchronicles.co.uk/rb/wab

23 October 2019 - PMQs

↳ brexitchronicles.co.uk/br/JQ

24 October 2019 - Boris' end game

Johnson makes an offer to give Parliament more time to debate the WAB by voting on it on 6 November. He will also table a motion to hold elections on 12 December 2019, which will allow a new Parliament to be in place before Christmas.

28 October 2019 – EU grant flextension

The third extension to Brexit, to 31 January 2020, is accepted by the EU27. If the WAB is accepted by Parliament then the UK can exit with a deal at the beginning of any month before this date.

Boris calls for a general election to happen on 12 December 2019 under the Fixed-term Parliaments Act, which requires 434 votes in order to pass. But so many MPs abstain that with 299 votes for and 70 against the motion fails.

↳ brexitchronicles.co.uk/rb/BF

29 October 2019 - What a difference a day makes

Driven by the Lib-Dems and the SNP, who say they would back a general election on 9 December, Boris tables a bill to call an election on 12 December 2019. The difference now is that it can pass with a simple majority of the House. However, it is open to amendments, which could complicate the matter as the SNP want the voting age lowered to 16 and for EU citizens to be allowed to vote.

Both amendments are turned down by the Speaker of the House and not considered. In a surprise move Corbyn gives a morning interview in support of an immediate election without conditions, now that no-deal has been taken off the table until 31 January.

The bill passes, with no amendments, by 438 to 20 – this is the two-thirds majority of the House as required by the Fixed-term Parliaments Act and it is the same bill that failed only yesterday. Why did the House not pass the motion yesterday? The power of the party whip!

↳ brexitchronicles.co.uk/rb/EG

The decision to call a snap election brings this first edition of The Brexit Chronicles to a natural pause.

This book was written to inform and to help you make better decisions regarding the EU in the future. Although the story is by no means over, the next Government will take the country down its chosen path, on a blind date with destiny. Cilla Black might have summed it up like this:

'Well chuck, there's candidate one who'd rather be dead in a ditch than spend a minute longer with the ex. No ifs, no buts, he's out the door, with or without a deal.'

'Then there's candidate two whose been a Eurosceptic all his life, bless his little cotton socks. He now wants to renegotiate the exit deal, and hold a second referendum so he can campaign against the very deal he's negotiated and remain.'

'And, candidate three. Well, what can I say, she's gorra lorra, lorra, lorra nerve wanting to withdraw Article 50 with no referendum and move on like nothing ever happened.'

'Candidate four is like a spring coil waiting to be released on the public. With a name that describes what he's all about.'

The decision is yours.

Be careful who you vote for

Some MPs are distraught that the election will be chiefly about Brexit and not the wider issues the country is facing. It appears that Labour and the Lib-Dems will be running campaigns on other issues, but all the other parties will mainly be talking about Brexit.

Whichever way you decide to vote you must consider who will work in your interest over the coming years, and not just for this one action of leaving or remaining in the EU. With four main national contenders it can water down the vote and result in a hung parliament, so tactical voting might be the answer on this occasion.

Let me explain.

If you are a Remainer then your best option is to vote Lib-Dems. They are the only party with a solid policy of stopping Brexit at all costs. If they get into government, they are prepared to simply withdraw Article 50.

If you're in the Leave camp, then it's a little more complicated. To vote tactically you should consider who your current MP is. If you have a Labour or Lib-Dems MP then casting a vote for the Brexit party might serve you better. If your current MP is a Conservative, then supporting them is more likely to achieve the result you're looking for. These parties must also negotiate the future relationship Britain has with the EU if they are elected.

Look for updates on our official website.

THE EPILOGUE

The EU was created to make war between neighbouring nations unthinkable and leading to a United States of Europe.

The Common Market, created during the Thatcher years, brought European countries closer together as trading partners. Its supranational nature was always the intention, leading to a federal state. A single currency is a binding factor and the beginning of real dependence on each other. In principle, a United States of Europe sounds like a good idea. The USA was created on a blank canvas. They had no transport infrastructure, no bridges, no rule of law ... they started from scratch. It made sense to implement a single currency and have a federal government that could step in when disaster happens.

The situation in Europe is very different. You are taking mature institutions and dismantling them to create a suprastate. Cultural differences can be extreme, but it is those differences that make Europe work. As Thatcher said, let the Spanish be Spanish, and the French be French. When you water down a people's identity then one day the wine grower's children will want to work in London and there'll be no wine growers.

It's not for me to say if leaving is right or wrong, you should make up your own mind. The facts laid out here will make you better informed and I hope they've opened your eyes to some of the truths about the EU.

What next? ... **Strike Six?**